Searching THE FAR *Horizon*

A One-Year Journey of Discovery from a Boy with Asperger's Syndrome

To an Asperger's sufferer, the standards in many aspects of neuro-typical people are like the far horizon; unreachable and obscure.

Sean L. Gallagher

*To all the people suffering
with differences*

This book is available at
www.createspace.com/3562322
www.Amazon.com
Like us on facebook
The poems in this book are translated by Andrew W F.
Wong, Wan Jingjun, Witter Bynner and Mark Alexander
Printed by CreateSpace, an Amazon.com Company
Copyright © 2011 All rights reserved.
ISBN: 1461024242 ISBN-13: 9781461024248

ACKNOWLEDGMENTS

We feel so grateful and would like to deliver the most sincere gratitude to Master Chin Kung, who has dedicated his life to teaching Buddhism, gives profound yet clear interpretation, and guides me and my family to the path of Awakening.

A special thanks to the editor and her team, who gave us much valuable advice and has made the publishing process successful.

And also many thanks to Venerable Xian Zhong, and our friends, Carol Mutnick, Alice Hu, Shirley Tam, Mei-ching Chou, Emily Sivarak, Sharon Lei, my Uncle Mark Gallagher, and my Aunt Diane Gallagher, who gave us tremendous support in the process of writing this book.

Finally, the most thanks to my dad and my mom who dedicated their time, money and great energy to help me complete this "impossible" task.

TABLE OF CONTENTS

INTRODUCTION

It is like a miracle to me that my son has finally completed writing about his one-year journey in China. It's hard to believe that a boy who brought home report cards since elementary school containing teachers' comments such as "a bright boy, but...disorganized," "does not work up to his potential," "is using reading to escape," "has little motivation to be part of the class," "does not follow instruction," "cannot stay on task," has now finished this big project of writing a book.

In the spring of 2009, when I announced my idea of taking a year-long trip with my son to rebuild his life after he had failed to hand in numerous homework assignments and was addicted to the Internet, even Web-surfing during class, almost everyone had somewhat ridiculed my idea. Luckily, I had my husband's support. My husband was the only person with a 100 percent understanding of where my decision came from. Because he is the only person who has gone through all the pain and suffering besides me during our son's middle and high school years. My son was diagnosed with Asperger's syndrome at the end of eighth grade, which surprised almost everyone, because he does not look autistic at all. He was actually in gifted programs before we moved to LA from New York. One of my friends recommended that we take our son to be diagnosed after listening to my complaints about my son's problems. She observed that my son had many similar traits to her son, who had been diagnosed at an earlier age. Once she told me that we were actually pretty lucky because my son does not outwardly exhibit as many Asperger's symptoms as her son. However, what she does not experience with her son is the "hidden disability" that leads to the extreme frustration caused by misinterpretation.

"Hidden disability" is a killer that produces a huge amount of misunderstanding for sufferers and contributes to their frustration, depression, even self-destruction. In my son's case, we used to think he had no motivation or was looking to escape, while he felt overwhelmed with information and would retreat due to his slower informational processing compared to the neural-typical person. We thought he was just simply "lazy" or too attached to the Internet and other distractions or demonstrating a lack of self-control when he did not hand in homework, while, in reality, he had difficulty extending his short attention span. We thought he did not pay any effort or even try when he could not learn how to tie his shoelaces or how to sweep up a room, while actually he was struggling with weak motor skills and poor body coordination. We thought he was lying when he denied things while the truth was staring him in his face, such as denying not brushing his teeth when we could see his toothbrush was bone-dry. We thought he was so rude when he showed some awkward speech or other socially unacceptable behavior, while he had no way to understand a neural-typical person's standard and lack of the social skills to start, carry, and end a conversation. Worst of all, we thought he was such a disrespecting, rebelling teenager when he mumbled or gave a "don't know" as the answer to any question he was asked, while he actually lacked the abilities in comprehension and verbal expression. The most painful thing is that he did not learn from mistakes even after he was coached seemingly forever, which had been puzzling me until I read a book called *41 Things to Know About Autism*, by Chantal Sicile-Kira, who points out that they are incapable of relating what they learn to themselves personally. It takes a long time, sometimes years, for them to get the connection.

The contrast between the talents people with Asperger's show and the disabilities they hide is so confusing and painful. Over the years, we have given up our dream of raising a science genius, which he had shown in kindergarten, earning the nickname "Science Guy" from his teacher; a pianist, because he played so well, even memorized a long Chopin Scherzo that impressed the tester so much, she held his hand looking for "mom" after he past the highest-level test in New York State at age ten, and gave a one-point-shy-of-full score with written comments such as "It's difficult to believe that a person your age under-stood this piece so well and memorized it (like a true professional)," "Superior student (all around)"-yet my son gave up piano soon after even he had earned such achievement and encouragement, having forgotten that piece after moving on to the next one due to his "hidden disability" of being unable to keep memories; a car designer, for which he showed an unbelievable passion, knowledge, and sketching skills since he was a toddler; an astronomy scientist, when he surprised a librarian with his knowledge during a program in which the children in the homework room interacted with an astronaut in Florida through a special hookup after we took him to see the Discovery launch in 2001. We had dreamed many possibilities of the "somebody" he would become one day when he scored high on the IQ test taken at Hofstra University recommended by his kindergarten teacher for the school district's gifted program, and when he passed the entrance exam for Hunter College High School, the best and most desirable middle/high school in New York City. But all these dreams had been painfully shattered one by one because of these "hidden disabilities."

When my husband and I received the doctor's diagnosis in 2006, we went through a long period of denial just as any parents would. However, when I think of all the confusing times we have been through, I finally calmed down and tried to figure out some ways to help my son. Those days, I put myself in my son's position and threw myself in a corner of the house and drowned myself in the past after the morning chaos. I remember how my son loved to go to school, but always made an unreasonable fuss in the morning. How he wanted to go visit friends, had playdates, but only performed "parallel playing." How he stood on the baseball field and Karate class, completely lost, and did not know what to do. How he could not swim in a straight line, and how he gave only a few strokes on pages of many beautiful drawing books that I bought to encourage him when I discovered his drawing talent on some random papers with incomplete pictures throughout the house. I remember a heartbreaking incident which happened when he was in second grade: I was shocked when his teacher told me that she "didn't even want to mention his name" due to his disobedient attitude. She explained that my son was told to put away a book and join the class, and the teacher made many attempts to bring his attention to join his discussion group. Finally, she took away the book he was reading and put in the shelf. My son stood up, got three more books, and sat down to read instead of following her instructions, as if there were nobody else in the room. My heart turned to sympathy for the teacher. I completely understood how hard it was; because that was the life I had at home, seemingly impossible to get his attention. Not until I educated myself with this spectrum symptom, did I understand that he was probably suffering from the "difficulty of transition."

The past memory drowned me in tears—the image of his helplessness, his retreating, his struggles to keep up in the school, his eagerness to fit in, and his confusion with the world... I felt so hurt when I thought of the loneliness that was buried deep down inside his heart, the frustration that he had with the world and no one believing, the lack of self-esteem, lack of confidence, and the depression that he had been experiencing since seventh grade. The signs included an eating disorder, getting obesity, often crying out "I am sad", and sneakily staying up all night escaping into video games and being exhausted the next day in class. Those days, when he was desperately calling out "It is too hard," we would think it was ridiculous because all the teachers said he was so capable, and so we scolded him that "difficult" did not exist in a successful person's vocabulary.

When he needed support and understanding, he got nothing but high expectations from his parents and teachers. His peers picked on him and called him names. Those days he was like a walking zombie with no awareness of his surroundings, but with more and more anger and fuss. Literally, he had become a person that could not be reasoned with. Just like Rodney Peete described in his book *Not My Boy*, when his son's preschool teacher told them that his son was "unteachable," I felt exactly the same way with my own son, not academically, but emotionally and rationally. We were so attached on the side of trying to fulfill the parents' responsibility, pushing him to the limit of his potential, and unable to detect his hidden feelings, for he did not know how to express himself, how to ask for help. When I got the diagnosis, I began looking back. I had no idea how he faced everything all alone. I felt like a sharp knife cutting through my heart slice by slice... I could not help but sob for a whole week... and by the end of the day, I would stand in front of mirror, force myself to put on a smiling mask, then go to pick him up, pretend nothing happened at all.

It was an awfully late diagnosis at the end of eighth grade; the school system could only send us notices when he was failing academically. We were literally on our own. Sometimes, I wondered, would it make any difference if he were not in a gifted program? I remembered all the school counselors, school psychologists, and even the district psychologist comforting us by saying, "He will be happier when he enters high school and meets some people with the same interests; a gifted child sometimes acts in a very unique way; he will grow out of it, don't worry." One school psychologist even told us they were very busy with the other end of special education, and that because our son had no academic problems, we had no need to worry. The other factors contributing to my son's late diagnosis might be the lack of knowledge of ADD/ADHD and Asperger's among educators. I remembered when I went to the eighth grade counselor, brought on by my suspicion that my son might have ADD or Asperger's, she laughed and said: "Mrs. Gallagher, I have talked to all your son's subject teachers, none of them think he has ADD. With more than thirty years of teaching experience, I've seen numerous different problem students, and your son has nothing near Asperger's. Your son has simply a motivation problem."

After trying all the advice the educators had given and still having the same problems with my son, desperately, I consulted her about my last option. I asked, "Should we send him to a military school?" The counselor said, "Yes, it's worth a try." And that night, when we told my son this option, he cried so hard, he did not want to go...

As parents, we were probably the last people who wanted to admit their son might have Asperger's, but after all the discussions with all the educators, we were the only people left to face all the problems. Deep in my gut, I could never picture my son in a military school. With all the heavy training and strict instruction-following, how could a person who cannot even comprehend simple rules like baseball or follow instruction in Karate class survive in the military? We finally took him for diagnosis.

After the diagnosis and a whole week of sobbing, we slowly pulled ourselves together, and started to set plans. I learned about Asperger's from all different sources, books, Web sites, radio... I tried to follow most professionals' advice, and started to act as an advocate for my son. Unfortunately, it was a total mess.

The biggest shock I had when telling people about my son's Asperger's syndrome was that they thought it was a psycho or mentally retarded disease. Many people started keeping a distance from us. One summer after the diagnosis, he was put in a tent alone at a week-long scout camp, which was a violation of the scout law and the buddy system, because no parents wanted their kid to be in the same tent with him, according to the scoutmaster. We thought about fighting back, but how would that help my son? This was the cruel world that he would have to face his whole life; even if we won this one, how would that make his life easier later? Swallowing the bitterness, we ended up transferring him to another troop. For those who did not stay away, they often thought that we, the parents, were the problem—either we were too strict or we expected too much from our son. No matter how we tried to explain, people who had no knowledge or experience with Asperger's simply found it impossible to believe from his outward appearance. The only impression they probably have is from that old movie *Rain Man*: the stigma of an Asperger's patient, extremely smart in one particular area, but incapable in every other area. When people look at my son, they think I am either crazy or sick. I am probably the only parent they have ever encountered who would label her own child with such a terrible illness while he looks absolutely normal. How can I blame them for misunderstanding? After all, there are huge range differences within the spectrum disorder; even the professional educators misjudged my son to have simply motivation or laziness problems.

After failing at countless attempt to help my son be understood by others, we realized it would be useless in this direction. We changed our strategy to helping him to understand and accept what he has. In the beginning, we struggled with whether we should tell him the truth or not, until, half a year after the diagnosis, my son came home from school on the last day before Christmas break with an extremely cranky attitude. I was very frustrated and thought as usual that he was angry with me. I was thinking so hard trying to figure out what he was angry with me about, but I could not get any clue. After all, we had changed our attitude 100 percent after the diagnosis, becoming totally supportive and totally patient, and totally showing our understanding. I just didn't get why he would still give me such a difficult time. All of a sudden, a thought flashed in my mind: did something happen at school? I started the longest guessing game I had ever had in my life. With his defiant attitude, I guessed every possible situation I could think of and tried to be as gentle and patient as possible to help him let his feelings out. More than half an hour later, he burst into tears when I guessed close to what happened: he was the only person who did not get any presents or cards from the holiday gift exchange among classmates. My heart was bleeding. I tried to reach my arm out to hold him, but he pushed me away. That moment, I decided to let him know what he really had and the unavoidable issues he would have to deal with for the rest of his life, instead of lying to him that he had only ADD as we had previously told him.

That "breaking news" moment went surprisingly well. He was so calm and told us it was his own body, we should have told him in the beginning. But following that calmness came a very bitter, sarcastic attitude. He constantly blamed all his incapability on his "Ass berger" with a violent shouting. As time passed by, my worry grew, my sorrow deepened; I could not imagine what would happen when he finally hit the age of eighteen and took off with all this resentfulness. We would be more and more powerless to help him even if we desperately strived for it—and if we could not help him, who could?

I decided that we had to do something before his "independence" age. Of course, it was not easy at all, because he would give up everything to go to school, to stay with his "friends", despite the truth of very little interaction with them and being picked on all the time since kindergarten. Most people think autistic people are not interested in others at all, that they would rather stay alone. This is not my son's case; he is so fond of people that he would keep asking to go somewhere, to visit someone—yet he would stay alone playing with his own toy or video game next to his playdates. Since he was a toddler, this trait had confused and bothered me so much, Every time, I felt I had to beg to get a playdate for him since all the kids he had played with thought he was boring or rude, such as grabbing toys from others without asking, not sharing, seldom talking except about his car world...etc.

In tenth grade, he failed an elective class after the teacher gave him many chances to make up his missing homework. He argued and insisted that he had handed them in, until the day he was caught surfing the Internet while I was on the phone with the teacher, and he was supposed to be doing his assignment and making up the missing ones. This stronger and stronger addiction to the Internet plus his "independence" age coming closer and closer, we finally determined a break from his school life was a must.

Most people argued that we overreacted. The problem was that they did not understand or experience their hidden "comprehension" disability. An autistic student, while they may recite any information they have learned, they have no clue what it means and cannot discern right from wrong; consequently they mess up their behavior or speech without any awareness of social unacceptability. Because of this trait, the environment is the deciding factor on what they will become, in my opinion. And the Internet, despite the incredible convenience it has offered our lives, also created the deepest, darkest hole that human beings have ever experienced in history and has left parents with essentially no control at all. Sometimes I would be surfing in this darkness, and often was shocked by how unbearable the information out there has taught our young generation. My son had been reported for improper conversation in his scout troop, and had been expelled three times from one particular Web site chat room for using inappropriate language. No matter how we explained to him that it was socially unacceptable, he was not sensitive to the subtle differences, and insisted that he saw it on the Internet all the time, there was nothing wrong, the only thing wrong was that his parents were "old/antique."

Parents with a neural-typical child who can be reasoned with may have not much to worry about with the Internet, but with autistic children, their stubbornness and lack of the ability to learn from mistakes can drive you crazy. For example, when in first grade, my son had insisted his spelling "Lincon" was correct after I showed him three different dictionaries with the spelling of "Lincoln." One day in China, he told me that he did not believe it even when his teacher told him the same thing; it was not until he was deducted points in a test from that spelling that he unwillingly gave up his attached thought. Their stubbornness is like hitting their head on a brick wall until they start bleeding, still not looking for a detour to go around it. For parents, it is just too frustrating and painful to see this happen again and again, especially in the case when you don't have your child diagnosed and expect your child to have neuro-typical performance. And with the irresistible magnetic force of the Internet drawing them to an unknown and uncontrollable world and influencing them completely, it is just too scary.

The years of struggle had left us with few choices; the only expectation we had now was to "raise a happy child," but even this, our only dream left, seemed so far away when we realized how much frustration and anger he had deep in his heart. But what else could we do? We had to give it one last try. After all, we were the only ones who would have to face and take responsibility for his future. How could we allow him to soak in this complicated, polluted, value-twisted world? In a few more years when he reached eighteen, it would all be too late. We felt like we were racing against time, just as those parents who have had their child diagnosed early race against the age six, when they learn that it is the most effective time to help their child.

The idea of taking him out of his current environment was to open another world to him, to show him a simple living style, to introduce to him different life values, to help him understand that "simple is the path to true happiness." My husband once asked me, "What if we failed?" I felt the pressure grow both mentally and physically on me as the time of taking off came closer. I wished I could guarantee him a happy ending, but I could not. All I could be sure of was that it would not get worse. At least after one year in China, his Chinese, which he had been learning since babyhood, should be improved tremendously. Yet with all the uncertainty, especially his lack of social skills, even for this simple wish we could only cross our fingers and hope secretly.

"Why China?" many of you may ask. For one thing, the language would be no obstacle for me, and my son would get great opportunities to learn this unique language. On top of that, Chinese culture is so profound and beautiful; its land has legends everywhere that are full of ancient wisdom. Deep down in my heart, I was praying every day that the ancient culture and philosophy would help him find the simplicity of self nature that he had lost in this competitive world. We were hoping to bring him back to basics, let go of the world that has exploded with information, knowledge, technique and the overwhelming fast pace of life; he might then make room within his heart to feel the compassion and kindness that our ancestors have felt thousands of years through their teaching. Hopefully, he would soften his heart and heal his soul with this wisdom.

The exploring of legendary sites and learning the ancient stories has proven my theory. As you follow the journey in this book, you will find that the wisdom from those legends and historic sites has shown a completely different world to my son. Slowly, he has broadened his view, opened his mind, and released his emotions. It is like therapy, only better. Through the journey, you'll find how he changed from a resentful, angry boy to an appreciative, grateful figure; how he learned that he is not the only one suffering from misunderstanding; how the misfortunes of others are often much more severe than his; and best of all, how he reorganized his mind through writing this book and gained some control of himself.

I hope this book can offer a new perspective of understanding Asperger's to those neuro-typical persons as well as educators and researchers, and give some ideas to those families who suffered the same things as we did in their long journey. As the official statistics point out, the growing population of Asperger's, and autism has increased dramatically, 1 out of 91 children were impacted in October 2009, according to the U.S. Department of Health and Human Services. It is therefore very important that every individual of our society educate themselves for these very different groups and show their support and understanding. Because the more understanding and support they get, the more accepted they feel, and consequently, the less frustration and destruction it may cause in our society.

As the ancient wisdom says, the universe is a whole, individuals are all connected; only when every individual in our society is happy, can real peace in the world be achieved. Therefore, each of us has the responsibility to help others. The first step will be educate ourselves to a better understanding and become more tolerant to those differences.

—By Elaine Gallagher

BRIEF INFORMATION ON ASPERGER'S SYNDROME

Asperger's syndrome is named after the Austrian pediatrician Hans Asperger. In 1944, he studied and described children he worked with in his practice who lacked nonverbal communication skills, demonstrated limited empathy for their peers, and were physically clumsy. Fifty years later, the collective traits that he studied became standardized as a diagnosis.

Some doctors believe that Asperger's is a form of high-functioning autism, and regard it as being on the mild end of autism spectrum disorders; its symptoms differ from autism only in level or degree.

Asperger's patients suffer from significant difficulties in their social interaction, along with limited and repetitive behavior patterns and narrow interest ranges. Their condition is usually noticed around age three or later. Symptoms vary, so no two children are exactly the same.

Children with Asperger's:

- Have a very hard time relating to others. This does not mean that they avoid social contact, but they lack the instincts and skills to help them express their thoughts and feelings and realize the feelings of others. Unlike the severe withdrawal from the rest of the world that is characteristic of autism, children with Asperger's are isolated because of their poor social skills and narrow interests. They appear to have disabilities with starting, carrying, and ending a conversation. In fact, they may approach other people, but make normal conversation impossible by demonstrating inappropriate or eccentric behavior, or by wanting to talk only about their own interests.

- May seem to display parallel behavior. They may complain of loneliness and want to be around people, but when they are with others, they may act as if no one else is there. They also have difficulty comprehending the concept of personal space or sharing and waiting for turns, and may do things like take whatever they want, disregarding whether someone else may be using it.

- Have difficulty expressing themselves or even asking for help with basic needs. In some cases, even a simple task, such as requesting a glass of water, can be such a challenge that they will try to avoid it even if they are dehydrated. Therefore, they seem to lack the motivation to solve problems, and tend to let things fall apart to an unreasonable level— which usually causes a big mess and lots of misunderstandings between them and other people.

- Have monotonous speech, or mumble and slur their words, speaking unclearly. However, they also may have a style of speaking that seems overly advanced for their age, using difficult vocabulary words and sentence structures, leaving people with a confused impression. They may also lack the ability to control their volume, speaking loudly in places such as libraries or movie theaters, and annoy those around them, often causing others to assume "bad parenting" as the cause.

- Are unable to process information on a personal level. They may memorize what they learn, repeat details perfectly, or do well in answering test questions; yet they may not necessarily realize how the information relates to them personally, which may cause a misunderstanding and result in perceived "rebellious" behavior.

- Have difficulty in generalizing information from one situation to another, or understanding the difference between what is public or private. For instance, it is difficult for them to differentiate between the behaviors or conversations of people like teachers and their peers, and what is appropriate in public from what is meant to be private. This can lead them to make the same mistakes repeatedly at a great social cost.

- May have memory difficulties. Many with Asperger's may seem to have a perfect memory when it comes to details, yet often have difficulty retaining these memories once they are replaced with new ones. For example, they may learn one very long piece of music and memorize and play it like a true professional, but forget it all after moving to the next piece. This trait causes them extreme frustration, and the "disability" disguised under their "talent" leads to many misunderstandings that result in resentfulness or depression.

- Lack of, or having abnormal eye contact, sometimes staring at others, which makes them appear rude, shifty, aloof, or weird. They also may show difficulty in recognizing social cues or "unwritten rules."

- Have difficulty processing information from the five senses. They may be bothered by loud noises, lights, or strong tastes or textures caused from extreme body sensory conditions. Some feel a "sand rubbing sensation" to the skin and cannot keep their clothes on. Some may refuse to have their nails cut, or walk out from the bathroom with shampoo bubbles all over their head and refuse to go back to rinse off because of the water pressure from the shower head hurts their scalp (using a sponge in this instance to reduce the pressure is recommended). Unlike blindness or deafness, those with Asperger's receive sensory information, but their brain processes it abnormally in an unusual way and causes distress, discomfort, and confusion. Most sufferers conveyed this as the most frustrating area they struggled with, which impacted every aspect of their lives, such as relationships, communication, self-awareness, and safety.

- Lack coordination, may have poor handwriting, or have trouble with other motor skills. Even displaying correct facial expressions and body language is a big challenge for them; this usually conveys a confusing message and leaves them social obstacles. The gait of an Asperger's child can appear either stilted or bouncy, and they are frequently clumsier than most, because the part of their brain that determines where their body is in relation to surrounding space does not coincide with their vision. This may lead to criticism by peers, sometimes even from unthinking adults such as teachers, through comments like "demonstrates slowness" or "has an inability to tie shoe laces," which encourage peer disrespect and can lead to verbal or physical bullying outside the classroom. Some researchers believe that most sufferers face bullying on a "daily basis".

- Prefer fixed routines. Change from place to place or activity to activity is hard for them; transitions usually do not go smoothly. Surprises, such as being asked to do even a simple task right away without advance notice, usually do not go over well with Asperger's sufferers. This sometimes leads to feelings of anxiety, because of the possibility of monochannel sense processing not enabling them to assimilate the information fast enough. They also show difficulty with following instructions for the same reason, which leaves them struggling to fit in and ridiculed by peers.

- The most distinguishing symptom of Asperger's is a child's obsessive interest in a single object or topic, often neglecting to learn about anything else. Some children with Asperger's have become experts on vacuum cleaners, makes and models of cars, even objects as odd as deep fryers, and may draw very detailed pictures because of the possibility they may have difficulty in seeing things as a whole. They want to know everything about their topic of interest, and will gather enormous amounts of related information. They may talk incessantly about it, and their conversations with others will be about little else but their favorite subject. Their expertise, high level of vocabulary, and formal speech patterns make them seem like little professors, but the conversation may seem like a random collection of facts or statistics, with no point or conclusion.

Many children with Asperger's are highly active in early childhood, and then develop anxiety or depression during young adulthood. Other conditions that often coexist with Asperger's are attention deficit hyperactivity disorder (ADHD), tic disorders (such as Tourette's syndrome), depression, anxiety disorders, and obsessive-compulsive disorder (OCD).

The exact cause of Asperger's is unknown. Although research supports the likelihood of a genetic basis, brain-imaging techniques have not identified a clear common pathology.

The ideal treatment for Asperger's coordinates therapies that address the three core symptoms of the disorder: poor communication skills, obsessive or repetitive routines, and physical clumsiness. There is no single treatment package for all children diagnosed, but most professionals agree that the earlier the intervention, the better.

An effective treatment program builds on the child's interests, offers a predictable schedule, teaches tasks as a series of simple steps, actively engages the child's attention in highly structured activities, and provides regular reinforcement of behavior. This kind of program generally includes:

- Social skills training, a form of group therapy that teaches them the skills they need to interact more successfully with other children.
- Cognitive behavioral therapy, a type of "talk" therapy that can help the more explosive or anxious children manage their emotions better and cut back on obsessive interests and repetitive routines.
- Medication for co-existing conditions such as depression and anxiety.
- Occupational or physical therapy for children with sensory problems or poor motor coordination.
- Specialized speech/language therapy to help children who have trouble with speech and "normal" conversation.
- Parent training and support to teach parents behavioral techniques to use at home.

With effective treatment, children with Asperger's can learn to cope with their disabilities, but they may still find social situations and personal relationships challenging. Many adults with Asperger's are able to work successfully in mainstream jobs, although they may need continuous encouragement and moral support to maintain an independent life.

Some researchers and people with Asperger's have advocated a shift in attitudes toward the view that having it is simply a difference, or even a blessing, rather than a disability that must be treated or cured. They argue that even though social skills and general knowledge may suffer, the genius that the Asperger's-afflicted may possess is a great gift. After all, Albert Einstein, Isaac Newton, and Bill Gates are just a few of the great men that are now suspected, although not confirmed, to have had Asperger's syndrome.

However, one should keep in mind that Asperger's syndrome, although it may birth "geniuses", does not come without great suffering. It is almost certain that those who are diagnosed will feel alienated, outcast, hurt, and alone, much more than those considered "normal". Even if they may have close connections and love for their interests, most of them also wish for a life of smooth interaction with others–at least, to "fit in" socially, if not thrive. However, for many, especially the ones who are not helped or taught and have to figure out social standards for themselves, this is a near impossibility, and their loneliness leads to depression and dejection. The suicide rate among those with Asperger's is noticeably higher than what it is among the neuro-typical population. Who knows how many great people the world may have lost?

—*Research by John K. Gallagher*

PART I

BEFORE TAKING OFF

PROLOGUE

It was 10:30 p.m., July fourth, 2009, downtown Los Angeles. Three good friends were walking down Ventura Boulevard, through Studio City and Universal City. They did not know when they would see each other again, other than that it would be a very long time. Although all apprehensive, they were making the best of the night they shared, talking, laughing, and singing. Passersby glanced their way, probably thinking they were drunk. It was cold, but I, the loudest and only non-Korean one, was only wearing a black tank top, having sacrificed my new button-up shirt to keep my friend Aaron warm. It had gotten drenched in the disgusting water from Universal Studios' Jurassic Park ride anyway.

"Man... I hate my house now..." I said. "All that ever happens is that I try to convince my parents not to take me to China for a year, and then it just escalates into a giant fight. Stupid school... I'm never failing a class again." Moses, the youngest of us, a Korean immigrant who had moved to LA only a few years ago, remained quiet about his problems, which involved possibly being deported back to Korea, and at the very least having to switch schools again, losing contact with the good friends he had made. He ended up only having to switch schools, but nobody in his family had an American driver's license, and suburban Los Angeles's public transportation is nearly nonexistent. The towns were also too big to bike between without getting drenched in sweat and taking at least an hour. "I actually don't really like my house now either," Aaron interjected. "There are too many people and all they ever do is fight... I have two cousins, a little brother, and my parents all living there now. Man, I cannot wait to move back to downtown. Walnut's boring."

Before I continue, one thing must be clear: I am just a person. A sixteen-year-old person, not that different from anyone else. A sixteen-year-old person with a lot of stories to tell.

Everyone has a lot of stories to tell, a lot of special experiences and memories throughout their journey called life. Some people are aware of them and some are not. Of those who are aware, some choose to share them—with friends, family, teachers, or anyone who will listen. I had originally planned on sharing my story after my experimental journey had led me to a better life, but I don't want to forget it. And in a way, I have already finished a significant chapter of my life.

GREW UP A SCREW-UP

"**R**etard." "Freak." "Suspicious-looking boy who is obviously up to no good." These were some of the nicer names attributed to me throughout my childhood, products of my frequent odd expressions and behavior. But slowly, things eventually began to change. In 2007, when I was in eighth grade, I was diagnosed with Asperger's syndrome. That would explain my low number of friends, lower number of points out of 100 on report cards, and nonexistent number of party invitations. I was on my sixth school, having left the first three and the fifth in search of a new beginning and better reputation and almost being expelled from the fourth for grades that even a community college would probably frown upon.

It was a regular pattern in my life: I got into the best schools and got the worst grades. People were interested in me for the first few days, then my classmates figured out that I was weird and my teachers figured out that I didn't do my homework or pay attention in class unless I was interested. Teachers were suspicious of me because I didn't look them in their eyes. They thought I was a thief, the type of kid who would steal and be unreasonably violent. I had been laughed at, gotten suspension and multiple detentions—and I had no idea why. I had never done anything exceptionally illegal, and none of my numerous school fights had been my fault. Obviously, the world was against me.

After my near expulsion from New York City's Hunter College High School, my family decided to move across the country to Los Angeles. My parents drove our '95 Nissan Quest, with me in the back seat next to a pile of luggage, from Queens to Los Angeles, in an unforgettable two-week cross-country adventure. Although intrigued by the sights I saw and things I experienced on that journey, my overpowering emotions were still apprehension and resent at having to leave my beloved New York City. From what I had seen of the suburbs of Los Angeles, they were too boring, too clean, and too inconvenient. There were no subways, and the buses and trains were expensive and infrequent. The streets and houses were newer and cleaner—they lacked the character of New York's crumbling, historical infrastructure, and the sun was always out. Never again would I truly have a white Christmas. How would I go skiing in the winter? I would have to stay at home all day, being driven around by my parents, instead of having the independence that I could enjoy in New York, riding the subway anywhere in the city by myself, leaving in the early morning and coming home at night. I didn't know what to do.

ACTIONS OVER WORDS

Almost every child that has Asperger's syndrome has experienced the same pains and misunderstandings that I have. But that doesn't mean life can't be better. With an extraordinary amount of effort, things can change. Maybe they will never be perfect, but significant improvement can take place. And that makes all the difference. I finally learned where all my problems were coming from in an epic one-year journey through Asia to find and overcome my biggest enemy—myself.

My mother was the one who saved my life. She had always been the most ambitious and accomplished member of my immediate family, determined and calculated, with a master's degree in New York after having graduated from the best college in Taiwan. She always had the ability to do perfectly any job that she wanted. She had helped my dad get a good job by making him understand the importance of looking people in the eye when talking and dressing to make a good first impression. And although I had many more problems than my dad, she was determined to help me fix them so that I would be able to live happily and in harmony with everything out in the cold world.

My parents had been considering pulling me out of school for a year after my eighth grade, the year I was diagnosed, but I never thought they would actually do it. I could take care of myself, and my grades had never gotten me left back. Besides, I was slowly improving—my GPA was at 2.83 now, much better than it had been for the past three years. And I had made a few good friends, who actually invited me places and called me just to talk. If I left school for a year, I would be bored to death, and I doubted any significant change would happen. Plus, when I got back to school, I would have already forgotten everything and would have to relearn it. Needless to say, I vehemently rejected the idea.

However, actions speak stronger than words, and when I failed another class, although only an elective, they had a perfect excuse to take me out of school and on this journey. I had to realize and face my problems instead of running away. I had to see myself for who I really was instead of blaming everybody else for my hardships. Through this year, with the help of many mentors and guidance, I would finally realize just what I had to do to change myself. I was faced with no other option. I felt that just when I had finally made a few good friends, I had to leave them.

PART II

HERMIT LIFE IN ANHUI

July ~ September 2009

SHANGHAI'D

We arrived in Shanghai around midnight, delayed more than a day by a faulty black box. We stayed in a dilapidated hotel provided by the airline as compensation for the delay, and the next morning we left for Lujiang, a rural town in the province of Anhui. Halfway through the taxi ride, the driver asked casually, "Where you guys from?" We hesitated. Poor Asian countries (along with New York City) had a notorious reputation for pickpockets and unreasonably overpricing goods and services to tourists who would be unaware. After a long pause, my mom answered, "America". The driver chuckled and replied, "Ha! I thought you were from Xinjiang!" This took us by surprise. Xinjiang was a very remote westernmost province of China, along part of the Silk Road, and to most Asian people, I looked foreign. Why would anyone think I was from Xinjiang?

The taxi driver explained, "I thought you were a Uygur. You look like one. Riots are going on in Xinjiang right now, and a lot of people are fleeing." After some research, we learned that the Uygurs were an ethnic group, related to the Turkish, who were native to Xinjiang. The Han people, the main ethnic group in China, had started to move into Xinjiang in great numbers, and for various reasons they have never gotten along.

As I looked out the window at Shanghai's dirty streets and buildings, I wondered what it would be like to grow up, poor and discriminated against, in a remote area with nearly none of the things I took for granted today. Forget the MP3 player I had become so attached to since my first one in seventh grade, much less the Nike Air Force 1s that I so wanted. Even my home and food would be hard to keep adequate.

Just then, a bus tire exploded suddenly about three cars behind us, and I snapped back to my present situation—scared, angry, and nervous. My situation was nowhere near as bad, but I still felt repressed and angry. For all I knew, I would be doing hard labor in a remote Chinese mountain for the next year, with probably no contact to the friends I had finally just made and so loved, being forced to learn about Confucius and Buddhism and other respectable but boring ancient stuff, and sleeping in some hut with no real toilet or shower.

At last, by taxi, train, bus, and tuk-tuk we had arrived at the temple that we would call home for the next month. The people were poor, the streets were dirty, and many of the toilets were holes in the ground. With more litter than New York City streets, the unpaved dirt roads had garbage from years ago fossilized in them, half-buried. By nighttime, we had secured a room for rental for the price of about $30 USD a month. And unlike most of the village, it was relatively clean and had a real toilet and shower. Although I felt a looming sense of boredom, I couldn't help being interested in my new environment.

The houses they lived in were like oversized blocks, roughly hewn from gray cement and hollowed out, cracked, and covered with a thick, uneven layer of grime. Wherever there was space, and a family with enough money, they had purchased the land and built their own house. Since, especially in rural areas, building codes were apparently nonexistent, houses were randomly strewn across the land, arranged almost on top of each other.

The cars they drove were mostly beat-up, cheap, low-quality models manufactured by Chinese companies. The oldest ones were perhaps ten or fifteen years old and looked "straight outta Compton"—at least if Chinese-manufactured subcompacts sold only in mainland China could ever be popular in Compton. Even worse were the tuk-tuks, also known as auto-rickshaws. They were motorcycles with the back cut off and a rear axle and wheels attached, along with a dark, dirty, uncomfortable compartment for passengers or farming equipment, including live animals. Fortunately, the ones that carried passengers seemed not to be used for anything else. They were slow and bumpy, but cheaper than taxis and interesting to experience. Unfortunately, our ignorance was obvious to the locals, and we were overcharged for that first ride.

HIDDEN FORTUNE

Hard labor was exactly how it started. The first day of my arrival just happened to be the last day of the temple's project to build a new water reservoir, meaning there were tens of sweaty Chinese monks, nuns, and stay-home Buddhist volunteers digging dirt and splashing muddy stagnant water out of a large, square pool. I started in the morning, the second person to start working that day, and left in the late afternoon. My mother, however, surprised me by joining me after she had finished praying and working just as hard, although not as long. However, while the work left me sore and tired, with no obvious benefits, my mom experienced something miraculous.

The job we were doing involved carrying heavy loads of mud from the reservoir to the river, a short walk away, and the loads were so heavy that they could only be carried easily by hanging them on a bamboo pole and having one person on each end of the pole carry it on their shoulder. My mother had had shoulder pains for most of her life that I know—at least since a serious car crash more than two decades ago. At one point, it had gotten so bad that for several years she was unable to raise her arm higher than her shoulder. Although her arm had gotten better from massage and therapy back home, but under the pressure of this trip, it had began hurting again for weeks long before we took off for this trip. Although the pain was bad, she still insisted on working together with us to volunteer.

But the strange thing is what happened the next morning. When she woke up, she stretched, and then, after waving it around a few times, exclaimed that her arm did not hurt anymore. Presumably, the bamboo poles that we used to carry the mud had dug into her shoulder, acting as a massage, and eradicated the pain.

In Chinese philosophy, there is an aphorism, "To take hardship reduces hardship, while to spend fortune lessens fortune." My mother's experience seemed to have proved this; doing hard work led to her shoulder feeling better.

That night, I collapsed, exhausted, on the bed. "This isn't bad," I thought. "At least I'll probably get a lot of exercise." I actually preferred working to exhaustion over reading any boring books. It wasn't that I didn't appreciate history and culture; I just found much of it boring.

Building a reservoir in a Temple of Lujiang, Anhui.

MAKING A DIFFERENCE

The class wasn't that bad at first. There were some people my age in a similar situation, and I talked to them. There was a girl my age and over those few weeks, we began to like each other. But it was a relationship that was destined to fall apart. There were just too many obstacles, too much distance. We had to go our separate ways when I left the temple and she went to another school in a different province. And the temple was against talking too much, even among friends of the same sex, so after the first three days, we were barely able to speak to each other.

It was a strange and beautiful place, but I felt detached from the world I knew and loved. My only communication with my friends was through text messages, and I had almost no opportunities to send any. I got up at 3:00 a.m. and went to sleep at nine every day, and even if I had time, my mom thought talking to my friends would distract me.

During our staying in this tiny village, my mom encouraged the villagers to dispose of waste properly, and not to litter, but they wouldn't listen. "The rain will wash it away!" "The sun melts it!" they exclaimed. They seemed to ignore the half-buried slippers and plastic bags embedded in the dirt road, and to be genuinely unaware that plastic doesn't just melt in the sun, even after a hundred years.

After countless fruitless attempts to convince the local people not to litter, she decided to lead by example, and quietly led me along the road near our rental apartment picking up every piece of garbage we could find, and placing it in the garbage dump. At first, everyone laughed at us. They still thought that our actions were pointless and continued to litter.

A few days later, we had to leave for another temple, and when we came back in a week to pick up the rest of our stuff there was a significant and obvious change noticeable in the surroundings, with almost no remaining garbage except things already entombed in the roads.

It may have been caused by other factors, but sometimes, one person can make a big difference. And every person influenced can go on to influence other people, so, although indirectly, one person can possibly influence thousands. My mom had done the impossible and proven that one person can make a difference in front of my eyes.

Although I was always familiar with the concept, I had never really believed that it was possible. If I pick up a piece of trash, or make an effort not to waste food or resources, the whole world isn't going to follow me. But the important thing is, maybe one person who sees me will, whether I know it or not. And even influencing just one person is making a difference.

OVERSHADOWED

After about a month, we had gone to Jushiling, another Buddhist organization in Lujiang, which had more kids and was less like training to be a monk. The schedule consisted of getting up before 5:00 a.m. for class, then doing volunteer work and watching Buddhist/Confucian teachings in DVDs. I reasoned, I was already there, so I should work as hard as I can and not just waste time, and I managed to earn some respect from my classmates when they saw me work. However, I also liked to complain, and this was one thing my classmates scorned.

Far more significant was the fact that I was completely overshadowed by my mother. I would only work during the scheduled times, but my mom, although adults didn't have to work at all, did the hardest volunteer work, cleaning the dirtiest and most uncomfortable places. Maybe her intolerance of dirty and messy environments helped her do it, but everyone knew that the biggest reason was to make up for my own incompetence and convince the owner of the organization to let me stay.

She scrubbed the garbage collection area, a spot that most people turned away from or hold their breath when passing by; cleaned a small smelly corner of the cement floor which had garbage and grime ingrained into it; and led the force to organize the storage room in the attic, the most swelteringly hot, humid place in the building, which had been neglected for so long that rats and cockroaches ran rampant, leaving their excrement and urine stains all over the disorganized, long-forgotten items. Although I knew and appreciated her efforts, the overpowering emotions were jealousy and anger. "Do you know how hard your mom is working to keep you here? And you still can't make more of an effort?" All day, I heard words of reproach like these. How was I supposed to do any better? I already did all my responsibilities...

Every night in the class, we had a session where we talked about other people's good points and repented our own mistakes. Almost every night, I heard at least one classmate praise my mother, although she was not a student in the class, saying that they had seen her working in the courtyard, or heard her say something helpful to somebody, or something similar. Along the months we spent there, they praised me maybe only three or four times. Although thankful, I was still feeling jealous and angry. And I still would much rather be in school with my friends instead of being overshadowed by someone that I already resented for taking me here.

TEACHING A MAN TO FISH

The founder of Jushiling was a middle-aged woman, assertive and powerful with a secure job. She had come upon Master Chin Kung's teachings by chance, and was so touched that she began to go to Australia once a year to see and learn from Master Chin Kung in person.

Master Chin Kung, a most respected Pure Land Buddhism teacher, has influenced millions of people all over the world, and is also my mom's guide in her Buddhism practice. The founder of Jushiling was fortunate enough to have personal conversations with him, and after a few years, Master Chin Kung saw her potential and advised her to return to her hometown, Lujiang, and open an educational center. Upon her arrival back in Lujiang, she immediately took a mortgage from the bank and constructed Jushiling. Education is the best way to help others because, if done properly, its influence can be infinite. Each person educated can go on to influence others, and spread the wisdom across the whole world. "Give a man a fish, feed him for a night, but teach a man to fish, feed him for life."

At Jushiling, people of every age could be found— there were young elementary-school children, adolescents, adults, and seniors. All of the children are girls, mostly orphans abandoned in front of temples because of the one-child policy in China. Next youngest were adolescents in their teens or early twenties, most of whom had already graduated from high school—some had even graduated from college. The adults and seniors had given up all of the worldly pleasures and comforts of living at home to pursue a life of Buddhist purity. In Jushiling, they were free to live as they wanted, as long as they chanted Buddha's name and practiced his teachings. Master Chin Kung's DVDs ran 24 hours a day in the lobby and a small room upstairs next to a large chanting hall, where people walked around as exercise and chanted Amitabha's name in the meantime. And people could frequently be found watching Master Chin Kung's teaching of Amitabha and his Pure Land intently in both places.

However, no matter where they were from, they came from all over China to learn about ancient Chinese culture and tradition. Some of adolescents had already been accepted by colleges and came from faraway places during the summer before the college started. It seems to me that they had been attracted by ancient Chinese sage wisdom. I think it's great to see how Chinese tradition has somewhat recovered here; as you may know, traditional Chinese culture and value had almost completely been destroyed during the Cultural Revolution in mainland China.

As students, our responsibilities were to help cook and clean, and we put in most of the physical work to run the facility. In the morning when the vegetables arrived, we prepared them for lunch, and then we cleaned the dining room and kitchen after meals. Dinner was usually a large pot of noodles, which we would also help prepare and serve. Porridge and a few different preserved vegetables, as well as a fresh dish of chopped ginger, was the typical breakfast. Every week, three different students would be assigned to get up at 4:30 to help the chef prepare the first meal of the day. The rest of us would attend a morning class at 5:00 before breakfast. Every afternoon, we also had a Tai Chi class. And Buddhism, Confucianism, and Taoism teachings filled the rest of our daily schedule.

UTOPIA?

Everybody at Jushiling seemed happy, from the youngest kid to the oldest person. The ancient Chinese philosophies place a strong emphasis on compassion and respect, especially for elders. We helped and supported each other whenever we could. Confucius frequently said, "Respect all elders as if they were your own parents or grandparents, and care for everybody younger as if they were your own children or grandchildren." In his philosophy, if everybody acted like this, it would be a utopia.

This sounded impossible to me, but here, it seemed to be a reality. At Jushiling, the young have a deep respect for the elders, always greeting them by their titles and helping with whatever they need, and we treated the younger kids like our own siblings, playing with them, showing them love, and teaching them whenever we could. As a result, everybody usually has a smile on his or her face—the seniors appear much happier than most in other places, and there are almost never any conflicts here. For those people, it was like Western Pure Land on Earth.

The way they blend three generations, combining a senior center and orphanage together, is incredible, and can be a great inspiration for our society and charities.

In today's society, frequently the elders live alone or in nursing homes. Living alone, they are less capable of caring for themselves and will always have to come home to an empty house—having nobody to hug or talk to in person, and having to cook and clean for themselves. Nursing homes or senior centers, while the cooking and cleaning is taken care of, are viewed by many as even worse.

Although they may not identify with many of our characteristics, elders like to be around young people and feel their energy. In many centers, they are seen as and view themselves as little more than a number on a bed, a spot waiting to be vacated for the next patient or "resident." It seems like the final stage of life, preparation for death. Old people feel the pain of loneliness perhaps more than anybody else does, as it gets increasingly hard to find others who remember that war, or presidential election, or movie, or pop culture revolution, and they do not deserve to be forgotten.

This is why, in Chinese culture, the grandparents usually live with their children and grandchildren.

There is an old saying in Chinese which expresses how the elder generation is respected and cherished for their life experience and wisdom. It goes like this: "It is a treasure if there is an elder under your roof." And Buddhism goes even deeper, teaching us that every parent is like a living Buddha, and it is a great fortune for the young generation to be able to take care of their parents just as they took care of us when we were young. Under the principle of Cause and Effect, it also indicates that how our old days will turn out will be decided by the way we treated our parents or grandparents. After all, no one can escape sickness, age, and death.

My parents have tried to invite my grandmother to live with us, but regretfully she turned down the offer due to her Western upbringing. I guess we are just not fortunate enough to practice the filial piety that the ancient sages have taught us. The only thing we are able to do is to call her at least once a week to see how she is doing and show that we love her.

CONFUCIUS SAY

Di Zi Gui, the Standards of Being a Good Child and Student, was based on Confucius's teachings and compiled by a scholar during the Qing Dynasty. Its principles and rules can actually be applied to anybody, young or old, respected or neglected. Its main idea is to love all beings equally, respecting the elders and loving the younger. Parents and teachers should be especially respected.

Although I agreed with and deeply respected the general idea, it was a text I began to secretly hate. Every time I would do something that displeased my mom, she would reference Di Zi Gui as her proof. If she said something, usually criticizing me, and I tried to disagree with it, usually by defending myself, she would tell me that I was talking back and going against Confucius's teachings. "Sure, respect is important," I thought, "but shouldn't I at least be allowed to speak when I disagree?" Sometimes, I just thought that she was completely wrong and I had to say something. Every time I would say something, then my mom would accuse me of interrupting her. I would keep trying to get her to listen to me, and the situation would implode upon itself into one giant cacophony of raised voices, with the potential to become hour-long arguments of screaming. Every time, though I knew it would only escalate the situation, my pride still made me keep talking.

One of the lines in Di Zi Gui states, "If, when you hear words of reproach, you become angry, and when you hear words of praise, your heart flutters away, then moral people helpful to you will not often be in your company, while people that flatter and try to take advantage of your emotions will be likely to stay. If you hear words of praise and are alarmed, and are thankful for words of reproach, then flattery will have no effect and people will not try to trick you, and more people who can help you will be in your company."

The sentence does not mean that if somebody says you are a good student or skillful or beautiful, you should be scared and suspect them of flattery and ulterior motives. But that you should still politely thank them with a smiling face and humble attitude, but also be alert and reflect upon yourself to see if you are really doing what they praised you for. If you are, then you should make sure to continue it instead of settling into apathy, and if you are not, you should start trying harder to achieve it. By having this attitude, the people in your company will not be scared to reprimand you, telling you of your own mistakes, because they can rest assured that you will not be angry and the relationship will not be damaged. By their advice and criticism, you will be able to fix your own faults and improve yourself as a whole.

After learning more about Di Zi Gui and experiencing its manifestation at Jushiling, I was able to appreciate it more fully and began to challenge myself to embrace it and embody its principles. I realized that arguing with my mom and interrupting her was pointless. Far more effective, I found, was patiently waiting until she had exhausted her breath and bringing up my point nicely after I could see that she had calmed down. It was not easy to wait, but I began to try to do it. With my new, less combative attitude, relations with my parents improved, as well as with everybody else with whom I interacted. I felt that Di Zi Gui had finally become genuinely helpful in my life. And I started to understand that my parents are the only people in the world that were willing to take the risk of alienating me to reprimand me in order to help me to survive in the outside world.

ROLE MODELS

Mrs. Zhao, whom everyone called Auntie Zhao, was a woman in her fifties. She was a diligent practitioner, and was extremely good at exemplifying what she had learned through her actions. Her most outstanding feature was her incorrigible happiness and optimism. No matter what the situation was, you could count on Auntie Zhao to have a bright face and smile, and she was always working hard to volunteer all of her energy to help the center. She would always praise other people, calling them Amitabha or bod-hisattvas; never complained about anything; and was humble and honest. Through looking at her as an inspiration, I could see an example of what I wanted to be, and how everyone should act towards others and towards life.

Of course, some of my classmates also inspired me in many ways.

Dao Zhen was a fourteen-year-old boy who, like the other students, had come to learn about Chinese traditional teachings. But he was not quite the same as the rest of the kids there—while everyone there was an exceptional student and worked hard, Dao Zhen was even more of one. He used to be the class leader, but due to some misunderstandings, he was demoted back to a regular student and the leader position was taken by somebody else. Although Dao Zhen had done an admirable job and did not really deserve to be demoted, he did not even voice the slightest complaint about unfairness or appear to be indignant. Instead, he truly and wholeheartedly looked back upon himself, and tried to find out what he had not done well enough. This was a perfect example of following Di Zi Gui—he did not argue at all, but instead vowed to do his job better and prove that he was worthy of the position.

Another exceptional student was Kun Kun, who was high-school age. After Dao Zhen had been demoted, Kun Kun was appointed as the new class leader. Although Dao Zhen had proven his attitude and earned everybody's respect, one could argue that Kun Kun was actually the better leader. He was more assertive and firm, and seemed more outgoing. When something had to get done, he would make sure that it was done. Even if the students were becoming too relaxed and getting off track of their responsibilities, he could still bring everybody's motivation back.

However, despite this rift and change of leadership, Kun Kun and Dao Zhen each still had the utmost respect for each other. Neither of them had chosen to change positions, and both of them did their own responsibilities well. Kun Kun did not brag or laugh at his classmates, and Dao Zhen was not jealous or angry with Kun Kun. Each simply did his own job well, knowing that his time would come and his position would be insignificant in the future.

Dao Zhen and Kun Kun were frequently mentioned in the reflection class, and the whole population had great respect for their diligence and attitudes. Even today, long after I have left Jushiling, I still look to them as role models, thinking, "What would Dao Zhen or Kun Kun do?" when faced with a challenge. Seeing how they acted out what I had always viewed as mere words that represented a long-bygone era, I could understand better what Confucius's ideal society was like.

PART III

DOWN SOUTH

October 2009

A GREAT RELIEF

Our original plan involved staying in mainland China for a continuous year, without leaving or changing location. The visa that we got in America was valid for one year, but it necessitated leaving and reentering the country once every ninety days, and because of our remote location, this would be more than a small nuisance. However, other people had told us that we could apply for a visa extension at the local police station, so my mother tried to do just that. However, at the police station, she was met by a surprise. The visa extension was denied, and the police officers seemed nervous. They claimed that we were supposed to report to them as soon as we got to our destination, not after almost three months of being in the country already, and denied that visa extensions were possible. We can only speculate the reasons for their behavior, but a possibility is that the recent XinJiang riots combined with our rural location in a province not very open to the Western world alarmed them.

The next day, we were in for an even bigger surprise—the police officers came to Jushiling to investigate us and see what we were doing. They interrogated us for more than half an hour, told us that any further moves had to be reported to them immediately, and that if we wanted to leave the building, to call the police station and they would send an escort.

The premise was that they wanted to protect us, but it seemed like they just wanted to watch us.

As we made our decision to leave China and reside in Taiwan, we gradually traveled down from Lujiang to Kaohsiung, passing through Jiuhua Mountain, Huangshan, Hangzhou, Xiamen, and the Taiwanese-controlled island of Jinmen on the way. During this short voyage, we saw some world-famous sights that made me begin to appreciate and realize how great an opportunity this trip really was.

"Finally, we're leaving," I thought as I boarded the taxi to the bus station. I was more than relieved to finally be able to leave this remote, barren city and the isolated temples. Hopefully, I thought, I would go somewhere more fun. Maybe when I got to Taiwan I would be able to enroll in school there. Most likely, neither the schools nor my mother would let me, but it was still worth trying, I thought. Maybe I could even go live in the school dorms. Either way, I was sure that anything would be better than staying in either of the temples in Lujiang. And no matter where I was headed, at least the next week or so would be fun, full of traveling to world-famous sites between Lujiang and Kaohsiung.

FILIAL PIETY

Jiuhua Mountain was beautiful. It is one of the four most famous Buddhist Mountains in China. Each of China's "four famous mountains" represents a different Bodhisattva, with Jiuhua being home of Di Zang Bodhisattva, who represents filial piety. Emei is the mountain for Puxian Bodhisattva, who represents practice; Putuo is associated with Avalokitesvara, representing compassion; and Wutai Mountain, Wenshu Bodhisattva's abode, symbolizes wisdom.

Di Zang Bodhisattva, in a previous existence, was born as a girl who was a devout Buddhist. Her mother, however, was not a Buddhist and did many bad deeds. She had a special penchant for seafood, and ate a lot of fish and shrimp. When her mother passed away, the girl was convinced that her mother's bad karma would lead her to take birth in one of the three evil realms. The girl sold all her worldly property to buy vast amounts of incense, flowers, and other offerings which she donated to the temples, and she prayed diligently, hoping that such meritorious activities would assuage the sins of her deceased mother.

One day, while she was praying, the girl thought, "Since the Buddha is all-knowing, he should be able to tell me where my mother is now." Thinking about her mother, the girl wept profusely. Her sorrow apparently struck a chord and she heard the voice of Buddha, assuring her that if she were to go home and concentrate on his name, her mother's location would be revealed. The grateful girl did as she was told and fell into a state of heightened consciousness in which she appeared at the shore of a sea. The Di Zang Sutra describes the scene in graphic terms, telling us how men and women were being devoured and tortured by beasts and demons.

Once there, she was approached and politely greeted by one of the administrators of hell, who informed her that due to her diligence and merit, her mother was already freed from hell and granted rebirth in one of the heaven realms. To this day, Di Zang remains the very embodiment and example of filial piety and her story remains for everyone to look upon and follow.

The character for "filial piety" is an ideogrammic compound. It depicts the top half of the character for "old" above the character for "child," symbolizing the unity and love that should be present between the elder and younger generations. The position of the elder on top also suggests that the elder should be respected and loved by the younger generation, and filial piety should be demonstrated at all times.

Di Zang Bodhisattva not only set a great example for filial piety, he also vowed that he would not want to reach Buddhahood until hell itself is empty of all suffering beings. His vow has become one of the most famous spirits to be admired and followed by all Buddhist practitioners.

The temples of Mt. Jiuhua on the mountain top were amazing feats of architecture. And the laborers who carried construction material up to the mountain, stone by stone and brick by brick, are incredible. I started to feel a little appreciation to my parents' efforts, but still strongly felt that it was not necessary for this journey, and I resented having to live in temples, studying Confucius and Buddhism, alone and bored. I was still angry about having to leave my home for a year, but I was beginning to feel lucky to have such a unique experience.

FROM A GRUDGING ATTITUDE
TO A GENUINE APPRECIATION

Following Jiuhua Mountain, we went to a world-famous site, Huangshan, also known as Yellow Mountain. When we first got to our destination, it was raining lightly, and the fog was so thick that absolutely nothing could be seen. Although we were disappointed and thought that we would see nothing, we had already paid enough money for the tickets and a tour guide at the hotel that we decided to stay and see what we could. So there we were, hiking up a cold, wet mountain, unable to see more than five feet in any direction, with tens of other people equally disgruntled. Everyone on the tour complained about having wasted money to go on an uncomfortable, wet, tiring hike.

And then we got to the peak.

It was still foggy and wet, but by this point, most of the fog was below us, and the mist was blowing and swirling quickly around and past us. It looked like spirits, like mythical beasts and dragons, like the famous Chinese brush-pen paintings that many have seen but few believe. I felt as if I was at the top of the world for what seemed like infinity downward. The mist and fog swirled around our heads mystically, at unbelievably high speeds, disappearing into the white, endless sky. It was the most amazing sight I have ever seen on this planet, and I immediately forgot all about my anger and apprehension, forgiving my mother for her crazy plans and believing her insistences that I was luckier than I realized.

In that one instant, everything about the trip changed. I went from a grudging, forced acceptance to a sense of wonderment and genuine appreciation for my situation. Seeing the amazing structures and paths that were built, all by manual labor, I also felt a solemn gratitude and sadness for the workers who had built them. The newest area, which was still being developed, had a path that floated above thin air, jutting out from the side of the mountain, unsupported except for thin beams hammered into the mountain. How they built it, we are still not completely sure, but evidently it was not easy, as the death toll was rumored to be in the hundreds.

By that night, when we settled into bunk beds with blankets that had not been washed for weeks, in a room with fifteen other strangers, not one person was still complaining about wasted time or money. The lodgings were only for one night, and who could complain about the moist, moldy blankets when everything had to be carried by laborers up and down the mountain? The higher the altitude, the more expensive the food and services, and any blankets washed would never dry in the fog, so in our particular hotel, they were only washed once a month.

The next day, we were even luckier. Although the sunrise was mostly obscured by clouds, we were told that to see a sunrise at all was rare, and as soon as the sun had risen, we were lucky enough to see the "cloud ocean" phenomenon, which apparently only happens fewer than fifty days a year. Combined with a cloudless blue sky, fresh pine-scented air, and vividly shaped rock formations, it was one of the most beautiful sights on this planet.

By noon, the hot sun had started to evaporate the clouds, and mist suddenly began rising again. Within minutes, conditions were almost as bad as the first day. The sky was gray again, visibility had dropped—just another reminder of how quickly, and drastically nature can change. Our luck had already lasted the whole morning, and we were heading back down by noon anyway. Although I was only there for one night, what I saw at Huangshan will never leave my mind. It truly let me realize how lucky I really was.

AN UNFORGETTABLE
TRAIN RIDE

Hangzhou was a big city, full of historic tourist attractions, expensive cars, and neon lights. We rented bikes and rode around Xihu, also known as West Lake, a large lake at the city's center that was reminiscent of Central Park in my old hometown of New York. There were boat rides, lanterns, night markets, and gardens, and we biked to many of the historic sites including Leifeng Pagoda, a pagoda with a 1,035-year-old history swathed in mystique. Although the original pagoda has collapsed, the ruins remain under the new tower, which has been built by the government, and if you disregard the escalators marring the entrance, it is magnificent.

That afternoon, we were still on our bikes when a sudden rainstorm came. We hid under a gazebo next to West Lake with tens of other people, tourists and locals alike, waiting for the rain to stop. When we realized it would not stop anytime soon, we ran to our bikes and biked back to our hotel, thoroughly drenched.

On the way from Hangzhou to Xiamen, we took a train trip of nineteen hours. To save money, we bought the cheapest tickets available, but we did not realize how horrible the conditions would be. The train was overcrowded and dirtier than most New York City subways, and when we got on, there were already tens of people slumped over in the chairs and even on the floor. The chairs had upright backs, at 90-degree angles, and very thin cushioning. There were food wrappers and waste discarded all over the floor, and people were lying down, sleeping on beds of newspapers in the middle of the aisles. It was noisy and there were a good number of poker games going on, and the spaces between cars were full of smokers.

We settled uncomfortably into our hard, square seats, but I could not take it and got up to walk around, aimlessly pacing up and down between the cars. By the time I got back, my mom had fallen asleep across our two seats, and, not wanting to disturb her, I continued to pace. At about 2:00 a.m., the train stopped at one of the stations, and there was a tremendous commotion outside. People were yelling loudly and banging on the windows, and I wondered vaguely which terrorist group was trying to hijack our train. Only after hearing a few minutes of shouting did I realize that they were vendors trying to sell food. My detached faux-fear and confusion changed immediately to annoyance and anger. "What the hell are they doing?" I thought, "Everyone's asleep. It's 2:00 a.m. for God's sake, why can't they shut up!" Strangely, none of the other passengers seemed to share my feelings, as the ones that were woken up fished groggily in their pockets for money to buy food and the rest didn't budge.

At about 4:00 a.m., I had realized that none of the empty seats I had seen before were still empty, and sat down on the dirty, dirty floor, put my head on my knees, and slept. In an hour and a half, I was up again, pacing the aisles until I found a single empty seat; I sat down in it, unable to sleep. Within the hour, my mother appeared and took me back to our seats, and I laid my head down in her lap and slept.

When I woke up from the most terrible sleep I have ever endured, the train was once again abuzz with the conversations and arguments of other passengers, and the practices of Chinese citizens and workers were, to say the least, unorthodox.

For one thing, the trashcan by the sink had been piled up beyond the rim all morning, but nobody had come to collect it yet. Therefore, the empty Styrofoam instant-noodle packages were spilling onto the floor, when suddenly a woman, looking to be in her thirties, came over with a small boy, probably around two years old. She knocked on the bathroom door, and waited for about five seconds.

What she did next shocked...nobody but us. She lifted up the boy, pulled down his pants, and let him urinate into the overflowing trashcan. Public urination, at least for small children, was not uncommon in China, but public urination on an overcrowded train into a garbage can full of trash? This was something completely new. Next, we were in for an equally big surprise. A few minutes later, the train workers had come and gathered around the trash can. Presumably, they were going to remove the overflowing trash bag, storing it for disposal upon arrival at the station. But this wasn't America or Europe, Japan, or even Taiwan. Instead, he started picking up trash and throwing it out of the open window. Not wanting to be scarred any further, I buried my face in the cryptic pages of my book and resumed stumbling through the passages.

A BREAKTHROUGH IN CHINESE LEARNING

During the trip, my mom's goal for me was that I had to learn Tai Shang Gan Yin Pian, a Taoist text. It was longer than Di Zi Gui but shorter than most Buddhist sutras, but there were a lot of vocabulary words, and learning any new Chinese text was already a challenge for me. Unsurprisingly, I did not accept the challenge happily. However, there was no way to get around it—when my mom wants me to do something I always end up doing it eventually. And the long bus rides, as well as this nineteen-hour train ride from Hangzhou to Xiamen, to my mother, were perfect opportunities for me to study.

Now that I was awake, I could hide no longer. My mother was becoming angry, so I had to read the text. However, once I began to read, I realized that it was not as bad as I thought. In fact, it was almost fun. A sick, desperate kind of fun, but it did not seem as tedious as it used to. I made it into a kind of game—I would try to read as accurately and quickly as possible, and memorize lines, and beat my own records. The once-tedious task had become almost exciting.

After five hours of reading, we were almost at Xiamen, and to my surprise, I could read almost all of it. I learned many vocabulary words, but not only did I learn individual words, I even learned how to figure stuff out by myself. In the past, there was no way I could understand something this complex in Chinese without having somebody explain it to me. Now, I was beginning to figure out some of the pronunciations and meanings of words and sentences based on past experience and inference from the text, before anybody even gave me a hint.

My mother was proud and impressed. Now, I had learned that even the hardest task should not be avoided but attempted with all effort.

CAUSE AND EFFECT

Tai Shang Gan Yin Pian, a teaching from an ancient deity named Tai Shang, talks about the principle of Cause and Effect; since it is so in agreement with Buddhist philosophies, it is on Master Chin Kung's list of recommended reading for Buddhist beginners. Although Gan Yin Pian does not mention enlightenment or explain karma as deeply as Buddhism, the basic principles are identical—everybody is ultimately responsible for their own actions. They cannot blame God or fate or bad luck for their situations, because it is their own good and bad deeds that create their luck. According to Gan Yin Pian, there are deities that live in or around us, keeping track of each of our actions and rewarding or penalizing us for them, in the form of shortening or lengthening our lives or changing our fortunes and wealth. Their records are unavoidable and it is impossible to cheat, but they will always be fair.

The things detailed in Gan Yin Pian seem impossible. In general, the consensus of the human race is that ghosts and spirits have never been scientifically proven to exist, and I was just as much of a skeptic as anybody. I wasn't going to deny anything I heard, especially anything holy, at least not openly—that was bad karma—but all the same, I couldn't bring myself to believe in a lot of it. The idea of spirits in each person's body taking notes of their thoughts and deeds seemed like little more than a farfetched fantasy created to scare people into doing the right thing and not causing any trouble or conflict.

But over the months, Gan Yin Pian had become more and more concrete to me. Upon close observation, examples of Gan Yin Pian's principles could be found everywhere in reality. Cause and Effect, the unbreakable law of the universe, is the reason for each person's successes and failures, fortunes and misfortunes. Through reading Gan Yin Pian, I was able to see this more clearly for myself, and I started to believe it. Perhaps there are spirits, perhaps there are not, but the principles of karma and Cause and Effect definitely seem to be a reality.

In the past, I could never focus on one thing. Doing a simple assignment would take hours, and while most people, even if they procrastinated, managed to finish their homework, I would get so distracted that I forgot I even had homework. As a result, my grades suffered and, left alone, I would probably fail every class I took. I could never finish an assignment or task—sometimes, even if I chose to do something for fun, I would give up in the middle and never return to finish it. But the experience in Jushiling, with the lifestyle that I saw as unbearably tedious, doing work and watching Master Chin Kung's DVDs all day, and the long train and bus rides where I practiced reading texts, collectively changed my whole attitude.

Now, schoolwork seems intriguingly interesting in comparison, and even if I find something boring, I am able to keep myself on task, either by challenging myself to do it as well as possible, or telling myself that the sooner I get it done, the sooner I can stop worrying about it and go relax. With my new attitude, I was able to get through reading Gan Yin Pian without a tantrum or too much useless self-pity, and that had contributed as a great cause to the effect of my better attention.

WAR IN PARADISE

Xiamen was another boomtown, bigger than HangZhou, and even busier. The streets were louder and brighter, and the cars were more expensive. There, I saw the first specimen of graffiti that I ever encountered in China, and the areas by the water reminded me of a ghetto Asian Venice beach, with groups of young skaters and various stores.

After staying almost three months in the inland of China, I had almost forgotten that China had an ocean at all. My impression changed here in Xiamen; once I saw the water the next morning, I believed what my mother had told me about China having water as beautiful as Taiwan's—around the small islands off the coast of Xiamen, it was beautiful and the most intense turquoise I had ever seen. It looked like somebody had poured tons of blue food coloring into the water and lit it up with sunlight, and the sky was bluer than any other Chinese city I had been to so far. It was like the Taiwan of years past, tropical and beautiful but with an urban grittiness and chaos that has already been all but eradicated in the United States as well as in most cities in Taiwan—even my hometown, New York City, was a touch more orderly and tame-seeming. Sure, New York City has traffic and street food, but neither one is as terrifying as China's. In China, the danger of getting sick off of germ-infested street food is only slightly less than that of being run over by a speeding car running red lights on the wrong side of the road. Amazingly, neither of those actually happens that often, and although we got sick a few times, none of our illnesses were caused by street food.

On the way from Xiamen to Jinmen, we took a ferry. But this was not just a simple ferry ride—since Jinmen is under Taiwanese governmental rule, we had to pass through customs. This was something we had known well beforehand, but did not consider when, just before leaving, we bought a bag full of expensive exotic fruit which reminded my mom of her time in Thailand after college, where she ate them often. We planned to enjoy them upon arrival; unfortunately, the customs officials did not care, and insisted that we have to throw them to a garbage can. Sadly, we had to say good-bye to our delicious fresh tropical fruit while we crossed the border back to my mother's home country for the first time in years.

Jinmen was quiet and small. It is a tiny island whose existence is lesser-known than many other locations, closer to mainland China but under the governmental rule of Taiwan. However, it was not like most tiny, quiet tropical islands. Jinmen actually has quite an interesting history—it was a key Taiwanese naval base during the time when mainland China and Taiwan were fighting, and has actually survived a few major wars and stabilized the political balance between two governments, though it is difficult to imagine a small island like this could play such a big role. There are still ammunition shells lodged deep into the building walls today, as well as active army bases. Although there are still active military bases and a large military presence, it is used today for training, and there are no current conflicts in the area. It was quiet and small, an old-style town with charm but not much to do. The main road, which encircled the entire island, was only a few kilometers long. Nevertheless, despite my thirst for a busy city life, I liked it. It had an inexplicable charm all of its own, like a paradise, and it was hard to picture that many major wars with the paradise we just left had occurred decades ago.

IMPERMANENCE

During our one day in Jinmen, we went on a guided tour, seeing pretty much everything "important," or at least somewhat famous, on the whole island. This ranged from naval bases to underground bunkers to the projectile-riddled walls of houses. Seeing the relics of past wars in real life made the many war stories and pictures feel so much more real. Although Jinmen is fairly famous among the Taiwanese, most people would never have guessed that it was the site of many past wars. This small, unassuming island had seen probably as many important historical battles as Gettysburg, although probably on a smaller scale, and with fewer deaths. Nevertheless, its legacy is very real.

One particularly interesting site, aside from the naval bases and museums, was a long underground tunnel that stretched across part of the island. In the days of war, the tunnel was used for secret travel, and there were connections to main streets and army bases along it. I felt like it was reminiscent of the secret entrances to army bases in Hualien, doors by the beach obscured by bushes and rocks. During the tour, deep into the tunnel, the guide had us all turn off our flashlights and feel our way along the walls, just like the soldiers used to, while a speaker system played sounds of explosions and gunfire. There was no real fear or panic, but the pitch-darkness was overpowering, and slowly feeling along the wall, we could understand how the soldiers must have felt.

One thing we did not anticipate seeing was Mrs. Lin, one of my mom's friends from New York. Her daughter, Jessica, was one of my mom's Chinese students, and we had had no contact to each other for more than five years after she moved to China to start her new investment business. Like us, she was just in the area for a few days, visiting on her way to mainland China. Our chance encounter just proves that the world is an extremely small place, and almost anything is possible. My mom was ecstatic at this pleasant surprise.

Moving from New York to Los Angeles, I had felt like I was losing everything I had built up in New York, and this trip to China made me feel the same way about Los Angeles. Maybe I would go back to the same place, eventually, but no matter what, I knew that things would change, irreparably. Meeting Mrs. Lin in Jinmen, although personally I did not really care, proved that the world is full of more surprises than I ever thought possible, and nothing is for sure. So never get too attached to current conditions no matter how good they are, but also never give up hope no matter how bad they get—everything will always change.

This encounter with Mrs. Lin had made the "impermanent" concept come to alive to me. This new concept had led me to a better understanding of life, and I had a better acceptance to all possible changes. As we moved from place to place during this journey, I felt it was easier for me to handle the transition; now I was excited and felt comforted to return to my mother's home country of Taiwan, although I realized that I would miss mainland China as well.

PART IV

MIGRATING EAST

November 2009 ~ March 2010

MY INFANCY VACATION
"HOME"

Although I had not seen him in years, Big Jiu Jiu, the title for my mother's oldest brother, was the only uncle of whom I still had a mental image. After seeing all my other relatives, my memories of them were triggered as well. As we left the plane, my mom gave me the usual short speech about how I should greet my aunt and uncle. I followed her to the sidewalk next to the street, and as she walked towards a shiny car, I wondered vaguely whose it was. Only when the window rolled down and my mom greeted my aunt did I realize that it was my uncle's car. Big Jiu Jiu had gotten a new ride. Although it was actually a few years old already, it was in immaculate condition and had shiny, freshly waxed paint, wheels, and tire sidewalls.

For the first few minutes, after I had greeted my aunt and uncle, I sat silently in the back seat, listening to my mom tell them about our experiences in China and comment on how the city had changed. But after a few hours, I felt comfortable and forgot all about how long it had been since we had last seen each other.

Big Jiu Jiu's house was swelteringly hot, humid, and stuffy, but it was nothing compared to the summer in Lujiang, where it would wet the cell phone from your own sweat in a few minutes on the side of your ear when talking. Besides, the house had air conditioning, although my mom insisted on using it as infrequently as possible, to save my uncle's money and electricity.

Over the next several days, my uncle, who was retired, drove us around to see many sights of southern Taiwan. We went to the ocean, a good vegetarian buffet, and many temples in the area; at one, we saw a pack of monkeys, the babies clinging upside down to the parent's stomach. I felt like I had reconnected with my uncle, and the memory of this small island that I visited almost every year in my young age was slowly coming back to me.

ORIGIN OF FASHION, JAPAN?

To avoid the trouble of getting in and out of China every ninety days, we decided to stay in Taiwan for as long as possible. But the problem was I did not have Taiwanese citizenship, we had to go to another country to get a Taiwanese visa for me so I could stay for longer than one month. Between Hong Kong and Japan, the two closest places to Taiwan, we chose Japan.

Japan was distinctly different from both Taiwan and China—cleaner, more organized, and less chaotic. Even the industrial factories and shipping ports on the outskirts of Osaka seemed inexplicably, unrealistically clean, and there was not a spot of gum to be seen on the streets and sidewalks. The taxis were black luxury sedans, and every driver wore a black suit and bow tie, and opened the door for passengers. Every car was right-hand drive, and every pedestrian and driver followed every law and sign perfectly, waiting for the signal to cross even if there were no cars to be seen.

In Osaka, it seemed that every child and teenager wore a school uniform, and everybody older wore a business suit—the crazy fashions and trends that are so popular in other countries which reportedly originated from Japan were almost nowhere to be seen. Almost everything was in a shade of white, black, or dark blue, but the city did not have the same depressing, melancholy oppression of New York City or many cities in China.

Our hotel was a tiny room, with a bed barely big enough and a shower and ceiling that I would hit my arms on every time I stretched and turned. But it had a great street view from a big window and one of those cool mechanical toilets in the tiny bathroom.

Once we got to Kyoto, everything was again completely different. The atmosphere was much more colorful and relaxed, not as businesslike and serious as Osaka, and there were a lot of tourist attractions and tours. There were also so many white people that it could have passed for Europe but for the distinctive Japanese-style architecture of the ancient temples and historical sites strewn around the city. The streets were full of people of every age and type, and there were young girls dressed up as geishas or wearing kimonos just for fun.

Unfortunately, our visit coincided with an international medical convention, so every hotel room in Kyoto seemed to be booked. Dragging our suitcases along cobblestone roads, we searched every hotel for a vacancy. Eventually, we settled on a traditional bath house—a bit expensive for our budget, but it was the only vacant room that we could find.

The typical Japanese tatami room, carpeted in bamboo mats and devoid of furniture except for a 13-inch TV and a small table for tea, was disappointing at first. There were two blankets and kimonos folded up on the floor, and sliding bamboo doors. But once we saw the bath, we were satisfied. Although they were public baths to be shared with all the other guests, they were clean and shiny, with a giant, angular black marble pool and six showerheads on the side, and free soap and shampoo. Now the namesake of "bathhouse" became apparent. It was a unique cultural experience that would be hard to find in another country, and we were glad that we tried it.

Overall, Japan left the impression that it was a juxtaposition of modern technology and style along with ancient traditions and architecture, and everybody we met was very courteous and well-mannered.

With this five-day stay in this country, we had spent more money than we spent in rural China for months. As much as we wanted to visit more places in Japan, we had to pack our suitcase and leave in order to survive a year in China.

LIFE ON THE OTHER SIDE

Shortly after arriving in Taiwan, we moved to the Dancing Cranes temple in Dancing Cranes (pronounced Wu-Ho), RueiSuei, where my mother knew some of the Venerables, and they had dormitories where they let laypeople stay. There was one giant room for male laypeople, consisting of one giant hardwood raised sleeping platform with a small writing desk and another slightly smaller level above it, while the female dorm was set up much nicer. It contained three small rooms with two real beds in each and a flat upper level to accommodate more people. They also got a mirror and furniture. In other news, life is not fair—females are always treated better.

It was an improvement from the accommodations in China, being cleaner, more comfortable, and newer, but still spartan, to say the least. My life in the Taiwanese temple consisted of getting up every day before 5:00 a.m. to pray, jogging outside in the morning amidst the rising mist, and then doing temple chores ranging from sweeping the floors to driving an off-road lawn mower with a locking differential. The gas-powered edge trimmer that I also had to operate made me feel like I was wearing a jet pack.

While living in the Dancing Cranes temple, there was also another man living there, whom I called Uncle Xu. He was older than my mother, whom I had previously assumed to be the most ancient of human beings still walking on the earth, and had participated in nine of the ten famous projects by Taiwan's former president to improve its infrastructure and bring it a step closer to the modern world. Like many, he had been born into a poor farming family, and left home to work in his early life. "As soon as the recruiters mentioned the factory having white rice, I made my decision," he told us about his childhood experience of how he started to work in a factory, and also how he ended up working for many famous construction projects.

About half a century ago in Taiwan, most people ate porridge made of watered-down rice and sweet potatoes, these being the cheapest and most easily available foods. Public education cost money, so only rich families could afford to send their children to school. It was common for children to start working before they had even graduated elementary school, usually in factories or, as construction workers, and recruiters from the factories would often go to small farming villages looking for workers. This kind of practice is still common in mainland China, and still happens sometimes even in Taiwan today. In fact, as I was living in Wu-Ho, I remember seeing a news story about a high schooler whose parents had both died. He had become a construction worker to pay for school, and was found dead in a river.

Compared to my life, this was depressing. I never had to work for money or was in danger of going hungry, and my house was always secure and intact. The hardest thing I have ever had to do was wash dishes, put out the garbage, and work in the garden. I felt how lucky I was to be born into a "normal" family in the U.S.—I had both of my parents, and both of them were extremely hard workers who genuinely cared about me and paid as much effort, time, and money as they could to help me. I told myself I should try harder to meet their expectations.

The Venerables at the temple were all very good to me, cooking all of the food, giving me advice, and even reprimanding me when I did something improper. Although I did not like being reprimanded, it showed how much they truly cared about me, especially Venerables Da Ray and Da Shen, the ones whom we had known the longest. They treated me like part of their own families. Most people in a casual relationship would not risk criticizing somebody for fear of offending them and hurting the relationship. The Venerables talked to me privately and gave me advice on how to change my ways, so I was—and am—grateful for their guidance.

After a few weeks at the temple, I met Master Da Hong, the abbot. Master Da Hong was a very wise individual, but he was also lighthearted and humorous. He frequently told jokes, but he could also be very deep, and often incorporated or related his philosophies to his jokes. He quickly became one of my favorite Venerables.

A few months later, I met Hwaiqian. Hwaiqian was Mr. Chen's son, a lawyer. Mr. Chen liked to come to the temple grounds on weekends to do his work on his cases, enjoying the beautiful scenery and peaceful atmosphere. After seeing him for a few weeks, one of the laypeople at the temple approached him, and he became acquainted with all the Venerables. The next weekend, he brought his family up to meet us, providing the most entertainment I had had in months. Although Hwaiqian was only twelve, he was the person closest to my age that I had seen in months.

A NOSE IS FOR MORE THAN DECORATION?

After staying in the temple for about two months, we moved out and rented an apartment in Hualien. The main reason was foot massage, also known as "reflexology". While it may sound like a joke, don't be so quick to laugh. Foot massage is presumed to be an Egyptian method of therapy that has been used successfully for thousands of years. Its main basis is that the feet are home to pressure points which correspond to every organ in the body, and that massaging or applying pressure to the feet can alleviate problems elsewhere in a person's body. The goal is usually to untangle "knots" in the blood vessels in the feet, smoothing out bumps and freeing the flow of "chi," or energy. The concept is very close to Chinese medical philosophy; therefore, it has been very popular in Taiwan for decades.

My aunt's neighbor was a young woman, barely in her thirties, and when she heard about my Asperger's problem, she told us about the foot massager, Brother Mountain. She said she had married and had two children when suddenly a spinal injury left her unable to walk. When all conventional treatments failed, her husband divorced her, and she moved back to her mother's house. Unable to watch her daughter suffer, the mother asked around and found out about

Brother Mountain, and brought her daughter a few miles every day to get her foot massage. Within a year, the daughter was able to walk by herself again, and today, there are no signs of her past injury left at all.

Brother Mountain was a reformed thug and retired truck driver who believed in Daoism. He claimed that a deity himself came down from the heavens to teach him how to massage, and that the deity's foot was as big as a coffee table. For the first year after he had learned the craft, he gave anybody and everybody that he encountered free treatment. After a year, he claimed that the deity told him that he was skillful enough to start accepting payments and gave him set amounts to follow, which were cheaper than any other prices we could find in the city. While all this may sound ridiculous to Westerners, most Asian people accepted it without question. Therefore, Brother Mountain's house was always full of patients.

According to Brother Mountain, I did not have any mental problems at all; no ADD, no Asperger's syndrome, and no autism spectrum disorders. The only reason that I had done badly in school before and shown characteristics of ADD and Asperger's syndrome, he said, was because my nasal glands were swollen much larger than normal, and had always been this way since I was little. My brain was not able to get as much oxygen as it required because of this, and therefore, certain portions of my brain were under-functioning. In fact, the problem was so serious that when I was young I had to sit upright to be able to breathe enough to fall asleep, and in kindergarten I had to have my tonsils and adenoids surgically removed. Brother Mountain claimed that he could fix my nasal problem with his foot massage, and my ADD and Asperger's syndrome symptoms would be reduced accordingly.

Having no other hope, we tried it out.

The foot massage was the most excruciating pain that I have ever experienced in my life—at least, in recent memory. It felt like the tool was not a rounded, top-like object with a smooth point similar in shape to the totem from *Inception*, but a flaming-hot razor blade that sliced right through skin and flesh and ground directly against bone. But the pain went away as soon as he stopped massaging, and when he was done, my nose had already cleared up significantly. I was able to smell without trying after the fifth day of massage, and breathe through my nose. Amazingly, my nose was for more than decoration, which I had literally thought was its only function for all my life. Due to the exemplary results, we decided to stay and try out the foot massage for the rest of our time in Taiwan, and my nose gradually improved. Now, as I type this, it is already half a year later and my nose is still better than it ever was before the treatment.

LIFE SKILLS

Hualien is a small city on the scenic east coast of Taiwan. Although by normal standards it is tiny; the proximity of Taiwan's eastern mountains to the ocean leaves very little room for building, and consequentially, Hualien is actually the biggest city on Taiwan's east coast. Its downtown is surrounded by fields and farmland which grow nearly any kind of produce, from tomatoes to bananas. On a clear day, the ocean is just barely visible from the mountains, as is the city squeezed in between. The distance from the foothills to the beach is a half-hour bicycle ride, ten miles at most.

After we got to Hualien, we were completely independent. We were renting our own apartment and had to handle all of our own needs. We bought most of our food from a small market down the street from our apartment, about a ten-minute walk away. It was known as the "triangle market" due to its position on one side of a triangular block. This was definitely no supermarket—it was more of a farmers' market, with farmers from all over the area coming to sell fresh fruits, vegetables, tofu, and other Taiwanese culinary necessities. By about noon every day, almost nothing was left and the farmers began to leave, so every day the harvest was fresh, picked that morning or the afternoon before. Therefore, the taste was noticeably different—juicier, more flavorful, and crispier. A shop across the street even sold fresh noodles, which were still soft and doughy and tasted eons better than the dried noodles sold in supermarkets.

To improve my financial skills and sense of responsibility, my mom gave me all of our food money each month and let me keep track of it and make decisions. Similar previous experiments had proved disastrous, with a disproportionately large amount of untracked expenses, but thanks to my mom's training, I was prepared.

Although I occasionally still forgot to record a purchase or forgot the exact amount of money I spent, for the most part I was able to produce an accurate plan and record every month, never off by more than a few cents. I believe this was due to my new habit of finishing my responsibilities immediately—as soon as I made a purchase or got home from the market, I would take out my little notebook and write the date, amount, and item. This exercise helped me realize just how expensive food is. Although we ate very simply, mostly just a few vegetables, tofu in a pot, and cooked with noodles, and very often we skipped dinner, but every time we went to the market, we spent about $10, which would only last about a few days.

With my own allowance and Chinese New Year's money, I continued this habit even after my mom stopped checking it. It truly helps illustrate the scope and purpose of the money spent, enabling one to review one's own expenses and plan more efficiently for the future. I also had much less desire to spend money. Even though it was my longtime habit to immediately blow it all on food and magazines, preferably from a corner store in New York City, I no longer felt the need to. Although I was free to spend as much of the $300 of my own money, I rarely did. The packages just looked too big, and I really did not need any food outside of breakfast, lunch, and dinner. I saw many 1:18 scale model cars that I wanted to buy, and I could actually afford to buy one or two, but even if I managed to get them home, they would just sit on a display shelf, serving no practical purpose. I considered buying clothes, but everything that caught my eye was insanely expensive. So in the end, I decided to save as much as I could for future expenses. Car insurance in Los Angeles is expensive, and life without a car in a Los Angelenian suburb is impossible.

During the stay in Hualien, I also had to mop the floors of the apartment and wash and dry our clothes. The problem with this was that we lived on the ground floor, while the washing machine and clotheslines were on the roof, five floors up. This by itself was only a minor nuisance, but having to do it every other day became annoying quick. My mom's idea was that she wanted to train me to learn how to take care of my own responsibilities. Presumably, when I moved out, hopefully to live in a college dorm, she wanted me to be the only guy in the school capable of cooking and cleaning for myself and doing my own laundry. Maybe I would get called gay, but having a clean dorm and good food would be well worth it, and undoubtedly, at least some people would appreciate it. However, I never made things easy for my mom; whenever she wanted me to work, I whined. Now that I think back on it, I feel a bit of guilty. After all, it has been a true benefit for my life. Anyhow, I can control myself and cooperate much better now whenever I am assigned any job.

Besides doing the laundry, I also had to help my mom go to the market and buy produce (sometimes I would go alone), and then help her prepare the food. After eating, I would have to wash the dishes, and sometimes we would clean the apartment together. During afternoons, I was usually free to ride the bicycle anywhere I wanted for hours. But sometimes my mom had to burden even my sacred bicycle riding with tasks—occasionally, I would have to go across the whole town (which took about half an hour each way) to the Amitabha Buddhist Society center, an organization mainly spreading Master Chin Kung's teaching which exists in many cities in Taiwan and the U.S., plus many other countries. The Amitabha Buddhist Society centers had vast supplies of Buddhist books, DVDs, and items which they distribute to practitioners for free, and some even offered classes. Since we did not have any other form of transportation, whenever my mom wanted to get something from the center, either to give to a friend or watch for ourselves, I had to bike to get it.

All this after praying and watching Buddhist DVDs for hours in the morning, It was a hard life.

Still, none of this changed the fact that I was lonely. I barely had any contact with people my age, and every time I rode my bike, I would gaze wistfully at the other kids, walking and talking and playing and laughing together. I was too shy to talk most of the time, but even the few times I did, I never saw the people I talked to again. So most of the time, I just biked around the area aimlessly, exploring, observing, drowning out the sounds of their laughter and happiness with the sounds of my iPod, thinking of my home and my own friends.

EYE CONTACT

Eye contact—or rather, a lack thereof—is one of the most obvious traits of Asperger's syndrome. If someone is talking and for no apparent reason avoiding eye contact, instead preferring to look down or away, it is almost positive that they have Asperger's. While people with Asperger's would not even notice this, or would at least find it normal, "normal" people feel disrespected and suspicious.

Growing up with Asperger's syndrome, I had never really been accustomed to looking people in the eye, whether I was talking to them or just walking by them. Unfortunately, most people expect eye contact, at least during general interaction and conversation, and my lack of eye contact appeared unconfident, shifty, or even dishonest to them. I did not understand why. Looking in people's eyes was the awkward thing. Why would anyone want to have people look them in the eye all the time? It made me extremely uncomfortable.

Talking didn't involve eyes; words were heard by ears, so why would anyone want to have eye contact? I just did not understand it. Except I couldn't go on staring at people's mouths or shirts or feet when I was talking to them. It was affecting my relationships and interactions with people, and my mom kept telling me that there was some sort of emotion visible in eyes— crazy as it sounded.

The only emotion I could ever discern was anger, and that was with the help of a loud, piercing tone and harsh words.

During this one-year journey, my mom encouraged me—somewhat forcefully—to start trying to look people in the eyes. I hated it at first, thinking this was impossible; eyes were so piercing, so deep. It was scary. What if I was too busy looking in someone's eyes and my backpack got stolen? What if people saw me and realized how weird I am? And what if I got hit by a bus when I was busy looking at their eyes? What was so special about eyes anyway? But eventually, I learned to appreciate it. Looking in people's eyes makes them come alive during interaction. I used to just listen to words and only understand the literal meanings, but now I can look in peoples' eyes and see emotions. The information I can "feel" from eye contact is almost double than what I used to be able to tell just from interpreting words.

Now, I have more eye contact during interactions, it is difficult to tell I am any different from anybody else just from that trait, and I am even able to discern most emotions that people commonly have. In fact, the only person whom I do not usually look in the eye is my dad, who used to be just like me. I guess it just feels more "natural" with him, maybe making up for some subconscious awkwardness we both still harbor about looking other people in their eyes.

MY DAD'S SACRIFICE

Halfway through our stay in Hualien, before Chinese New Year in February, my dad came to visit us. Because he does not speak Chinese, we had to go the Chiang-Kai-Shek International Airport, in Taoyuan, near Taipei, to pick him up. It was a welcome relief from our daily routine of praying and watching DVDs, and I was excited to see my dad for the first time in more than six months. Before we picked up my dad, we went to my second auntie's new apartment, which was in the same city, and in the same apartment building as the apartment of her son, my cousin.

My cousin was in his mid-thirties, and was married with two kids, Jerry and Chen Yi. They were both around kindergarten age, and they were the cutest little kids that I had ever seen. They came with us to pick up my dad, at which time it was strangely dark and rainy, not monsoon-status, but significantly more than a drizzle. My nephew and niece, as always, were loud and hyper, arguing with each other and making a lot of noise. As my dad came out of the terminal, we barely recognized him. He was unshaven and had on a button-up shirt and pants, the effect heavily overpowered by the bright green windbreaker. It is a long trip from LA to Taiwan, and I could feel his exhaustion.

I could not wipe the smile off my face once I saw him. I hugged him and in a few minutes, we were talking enthusiastically to each other. My nephew and niece, on the other hand, had fallen uncharacteristically silent, and stayed that way for the whole twenty-minute ride back. They were not sleeping, either—I could see their eyes open. Our theory was that, having never seen a foreigner before, they were intimidated. By the next day, however, they were as outgoing with my dad as they were with anyone.

After a few days in Taoyuan, we headed back to Hualien to show my dad our apartment, a modern, white, square building with white marble floors and a colorful interior, which had previously been a home-stay. We also visited some old friends, my mom's family and Hualien's scenery. Due to its intense beauty, my parents noted it as a possible future retirement location.

To let my dad experience what we had been through, we encouraged him to let Brother Mountain check his health condition. Brother Mountain declared that my dad had a minor cholesterol prob-lem, plus an old back pain issue. My dad was forced to sit on the massage chair. During those fifteen minutes, all he could say was a pained "Where's...my...beer?" My mom told me to let him hold my hand, and he squeezed my hand so tight, it almost broke my bone. Asian tradition does not usually believe in painkillers or drugs, because they desensitize and ultimately dam-age the body. My dad, not being Asian, thought this was crazy and could barely endure the massages.

Not wanting to spend too long revisiting old sights in Hualien County, we went on a long drive and visited a waterfall near the southern edge of Hualien. We took my dad to visit Wu-Ho temple on the way, the one we had stayed at in Rueisuei, and introduced him to the Venerables there. Sadly, he was not fortunate enough to see Master Da Hong, as the Master had some teaching classes in other cities during the time my dad was in Taiwan, and none of the cities in our schedule were even close to each other.

We went out to some of the nearby attractions after the visit, these included beautiful hiking trails with magnificent rushing waterfalls, which clashed beautifully with the rocks and spewed streams of white mist up into the endless sky. As I hiked, I contemplated my dad's decision and sacrifice. To support my mother's crazy plan and enable me to become a better person, he had sacrificed a full year of companionship, housekeeping, and hot food, not to mention people to take care of him when he was sick, which happened a few times during the year. He had gone back to living the lonely life of a single man, living alone and caring for himself. This is truly the biggest sacrifice a father can make—virtually losing his wife and son for a full year. Our only contact was through phone calls and the two times he came to visit us.

Seeing the waterfalls and empty sky reminded me even more of how solitude felt. I remembered when I was in seventh grade, there was a few months' time when my dad was away to LA for his new job, and I had to go home to an empty house instead of his office in Manhattan. It was one of the loneliest times of my life. And even during that time, my mom was still there for me, she just came home from her work a few hours later than I did and didn't have much energy to stay up too long. It is truly hard for me to imagine how my father had to come home every day from work to an empty house with nothing waiting for him at all. I finally had a real appreciation for how much he must have cared about me, to let us go on this trip. A pack of monkeys clambering into sight on the rocks far below, reminded me further of how important family is and how much my dad must really love me.

VOLCANIC TOFU

After hiking, we went to a small town we had recently seen on TV, Luoshan, which was featured as a tourist destination. Its main attraction was that some of the households made and sold volcanic tofu. Volcanic tofu, you ask? It was so called because the tofu was made with the mud from the local volcano as its solidifying ingredient, one of two active mud volcanoes in southern Taiwan. Tofu is made of soybeans and water, and the quality of the water greatly affects the final product. The mud volcano water was rich in nutrients, but also pure and clean, and with a unique earthy flavor. This one household where we had our volcanic tofu grew all of the soybeans and made all of the tofu by themselves—there was no processing, packaging, or manufacturing involved at all. When I bit into it, it tasted much like regular tofu, but with a somewhat different, distinct texture and flavor. It was denser and somewhat stickier than regular tofu, but with a cleaner, lighter flavor. It was certainly unique, although maybe not worth the almost-double price. But again, it is something that you cannot get anywhere else.

In today's world, the competitive economy has endangered the Earth. Following the industrial revolution, the human race lost its simplicity and began to live in the most wasteful lifestyle in history. To satisfy the growing population and its demands, scientists and businesses have raced to create more "efficient" ways to feed the world market, many of which use various chemicals, creating a significant, unarguably dangerous, amount of pollution.

Although there are many different kinds of pollution and effects, there is one in particular that affects us most directly, but its influence is so surreptitious that not many people are even aware of it. My mother always suspected that the food I ate every day had a big influence on my sinus and gastrointestinal problems. As we resided in temples and remote villages during this trip, I could not buy any of the prepackaged, mass-produced food that is so easily accessible and popular in cities—not only processed food, but chain restaurants which get ingredients from central factories. Instead, we were only able to eat locally grown fruit and vegetables that were freshly delivered and cooked every day. As a result, the food we consumed was pure and unaltered, far healthier than the preservative and pesticide-tainted foods prevalent in most big cities. Surprising to me, my sinus became much clearer and my gastrointestinal also improved.

In Chinese medical theory, when we consume something detrimental to our body, our internal organs, particularly the liver and kidney, will work to expel the poisons ingested. This can be through the skin (in the form of pimples or zits), sweat, or excrement. However, when there is too much poison, the organs are overwhelmed and cannot process all of the waste. In this case, there will be abnormalities in the body such as rashes, hives, or, in my case, swollen sinus glands, which was suspected by my reflexologist to be responsible for my Asperger's symptoms.

The Chinese also believe that the most healthy diet is food that is *locally grown* and *in season.* They believe nature will produce enough nutrition for the creatures that live in its land; therefore, there is no need to eat food that is imported from other places. In other words, complying with nature is the best and simplest way to our health. By eating locally grown food, not only will preservatives or wax on fruit and vegetables be unnecessary, but the need for transportation of food will also be reduced significantly, reducing pollution and emissions.

As we practiced our "simple" lifestyle, I began to see its merits. Although I still did not accept such an ascetic lifestyle, I wondered, "Maybe this is really how we were meant to live all along." Just like the volcanic tofu, back to basics, pure, unaltered, and natural.

THE HIDDEN JEWELS

Taiwan is a small island with a mountain range running down the center, causing a division between east and west. It is said that the most beautiful scenery in Taiwan can be seen driving through the mountains to cross to the other side. We had never done that in my many visits since I was a baby. Now, it seemed to be a perfect chance to do something completely different: drive through the central mountains of Taiwan, into the heights of Taroko Gorge and the remote Wuling Farmland.

It was a completely new experience—we had never ventured this far into the mountains of Taiwan before. Amazingly, Taiwan does have snow in its high mountains, which are surprisingly large. As we drove up the twisty, narrow road, we ascended higher and higher, eventually disappearing into the clouds. For miles, we were unable to see more than twenty feet in front of us, a dangerously short distance for such a narrow, sinuous road. There were at least two times when we almost crashed into other cars, and many times when we had to stop abruptly and back up to let oncoming traffic through. Eventually, we emerged from the top of the clouds, and it felt like we were at the top of the world. The clouds floated, hundreds of feet below us, lazily above the faces of the mountains. Humongous orchards of pear trees sprawled above and below us, with farmers stooping among them, taking care of the plants and bearing heavy baskets of pears half the size of a human head. I could never have imagined farming on this scale at such an altitude deeply in the mountains until I saw it with my own eyes. It is just incredible how they created this miracle.

The road cutting through the steepest part of Taiwan's mountains, along with the farms scattered on the slope, were established by a group of retired soldiers, led by the son of Chiang Kai-Shek, Jiang Jin Guo. Many of the soldiers were in Taiwan alone due to the political separation for decades between two governments, with their families still in mainland China, and this project gave the ones who chose to help with it a great outlet to work to their potential, as well as a place to see and interact with fellow soldiers after their retirement. Although many people died during this project, it was considered a great success, accomplishing its goal of unifying Taiwan's two coasts. The scenery is so beautiful that central Taiwan's mountains are a popular travel destination and considered the "Hidden Jewel of Taiwan." The men who sacrificed their lives to help unify Taiwan are still remembered and honored today.

Sometimes in life, we feel like we have come to the end of the road, and continuing is helpless and hopeless. But all of a sudden, another way is illuminated, and we figure out how to overcome our obstacles. In the Bible, it says, "When a door is closed, God will open a window for you." And in Buddhism, all sentient beings are said to have the hidden jewel, the same nature and "powers" as Buddha himself, which are deep inside of us and only inhibited and obscured by our "poisons," such as greed, anger, ignorance, and pride. As long as we practice the eradication of these evils, we will be able to recover our "Buddha Nature" and unlock our true potential abilities.

Through Master Chin Kung's teachings, my mom tried to lead me to purify my mind, letting go of these poisons and relax from the fast pace, pressure, and technology of today's life. Although it was not easy or fast, I gradually began to feel the effects—my memory was getting better, my interactions with others improved, and things seemed easier to comprehend. According to the teachings of Buddhism, by purifying my mind, I was uncovering my "Buddha Nature." It was like finding a "hidden jewel" in my own mind.

SEVEN YEARS IN TIBET?

Although it seemed like forever, once the time came to leave Hualien, I felt like it had come too fast. The expression "one always wants what one cannot have" proved true once again—for the whole time in Hualien, all I really wanted to do was get out, go back to my regular life, but when the time came, I wished it would last longer. My mom's words strangely appeared in my ear, "Don't pursue the rainbow in the sky and step on the roses by your feet. Pull yourself down to the earth and cherish the moment you own instead of pursuing something unreachable." I guess my mom is right: a sense of loss occurred to me. I wondered if I would have learned more had I understood this concept earlier.

As my time in Taiwan came to a close, I felt a significant change in my conscience besides the sense of loss. I was happier, more at peace, and in control of my life. Faced with leaving Hualien, my most frequent vacation destination since infancy and home to many family members, I was surprisingly unaffected. There would be other chances in the future, and there was still the whole world to see. I had for the most part enjoyed my time here, but when I finally began the long journey back home, trekking again across many provinces in China's southwestern regions, it was a welcome relief and an exciting expectation. It wasn't exactly seven years in Tibet, but it certainly felt like it.

PART V

SOUTH OF
THE BORDER

April 2010

A CONNECTION WITH
MY MOTHER

On March 31, at approximately 9:00 p.m., we arrived in Hong Kong. It was a sprawling urban metropolis spread out among two main islands and one peninsula, with towering skyscrapers, fast cars, and busy people. As soon as we could, we took a train and taxi to our hotel, where we were greeted by a tiny room with two dwarf-sized beds and a computer-sized TV. The room was small, but it seemed slightly bigger than the one we stayed in in Japan—at least I could stand up in the shower. We were exhausted after the long journey, so we fell asleep right after a quick shower.

The next day, we set off to visit the giant Buddha on Lantau Island. Looking around we observed that everyone drove like they were racing, even the bus drivers, and on our search for the subway, most people walked as if they were in a big hurry and ignored our asking for directions, except for three very nice locals who helped and guided us to the subway station. They spoke Cantonese instead of Mandarin, and most of the people that spoke Mandarin had a strong accent, so communication was difficult at times. However, we managed to get there at about 9:30, upon which we began to tour Lantau Island, visiting the giant Buddha which was built in 1997 when Hong Kong returned to China from England's hundred-year lease. The giant

Buddha faces China, symbolizing looking forward to the reunion with China.

The giant Buddha is a great symbol of the devotion and hard work of Buddhists, and shows how magnificent and amazing Buddha is. It overlooks Hong Kong like a divine guard, and the sight of it is enough to instill a sense of magnificent wonder in anybody. When I saw the giant Buddha, shrouded in swirling clouds of fog, it was almost magical—his head seemed to reach up into the heavens themselves. I immediately felt a great respect for the people who had worked so hard to design and build him, as well as for Buddha himself and the sacrifices he made to attain enlightenment and educate us.

After visiting the giant Buddha, we went hiking around the old fishing village of Tai O, known as the "Venice of Hong Kong." Tai O, while nowhere close to Venice, did share some of its features—such as canals running through a significant part of the small village—but the small size of the village was nothing compared to Venice. All the same, it had all of Venice's charm, delivered differently. It was full of fish markets and other unique Chinese cultural trademarks, and Cantonese was being spoken loudly in every corner and street. Hiking the alleys and sidewalks of Tai O, I felt happy and felt a connection with my mother. As we slowly began to move past the clamor and commotion of downtown, things began to get quieter. Outside the boundaries of the markets, there were fewer people, and the surroundings were more benign and older. Rusty bicycles were scattered around the sidewalks, and the paint on the fences was so old, it was blistering and peeling like lichens. We were now able to see the beach from a different perspective, and from here, even the village itself looked silent. There were a few houses with narrow alleyways in between them, propped up over the beach. The water was gray, like much of the sky, but it was not for swimming, anyway.

We kept moving, and came to a path going up a large hill. With nowhere better to go, we hiked up it. From the top, we could see areas scarred by fire, ships drifting by, coast guard speedboats zipping past, the occasional fish or seagull, and the rolling, yellowed grassy hills of the island itself. The only thing we did not see were the dolphins that lived in the area. The sky here was blue and sunny, and it was hot, but there was an occasional cool breeze. Coming to a gazebo on top of the hill, we lay down on the benches, exhausted, and slept for more than an hour. Here, it was completely deserted. I fell asleep watching two hawks encircle each other, flying high and low, near and far, in the sky.

The Giant Buddha in Lantau Island, Hong Kong.

ALMOST MISSED A TREASURE

At about 7:30 p.m., we finally made it back to the hotel alive, picked up our luggage, and headed for Macao. The last ferry was at 10:30, so we knew we had a lot of time. When we got to the ferry terminal, it was just past 8:00, but a strange man in a suit began to speak rapidly in Cantonese to us and wildly gesticulate with his hands. From what we could understand, he said that the last ferry was at 8:00 p.m. so we had just missed it and we had to take a taxi to Hong Kong's main ferry terminal. He offered to hook us up with a taxi for $200 HKD—about $28 USD.

This is where the maxim "don't panic" comes into play. The proposition of being stuck for another night in all-too-expensive Hong Kong with four heavy suitcases and no hotel was alarming, but the last ferry was supposed to be at 10:30! We specifically checked with the hotel front desk before we left. Who was this guy, anyway? The lack of a uniform, the fake Rolex on his wrist, the eagerness to pull us onto a ride—it all seemed a bit suspicious. Thinking that it was always wise to make sure, we went up to the ferry terminal and found that there were still five more ferries that night. Due to our calmness and discretion, we saved time and at least $200HKD. We were able to make it onto the 8:30 ferry, and departed Hong Kong by 8:40.

Our ferry was delayed for almost two hours due to the heavy fog. The brightly lit cities were completely obscured. When we were finally docked, it was already past midnight. We booked the cheapest hotel we could find in the ferry terminal, and took a free shuttle directly to it. For those unfamiliar, Macao was a Portuguese colony in the late 1800s and early 1900s and is now an independent government under the Republic of China. Today, it is like the European-style Las Vegas of Asia—casinos everywhere, surrounded by cobblestone pathways and Portuguese-style architecture and ruins. Therefore, most of the official hotels here were very nice, five-star style, and owned casinos. Our hotel was called the New Century, a Greek mythology–themed waterfront hotel/casino, and for the agent's $750 MOD price (just under $100 USD), it was incredible.

There was a view, two large beds, a clean marble-finished bathroom, flat-screen TV, large writing desk and armchair, and overpriced sodas and Heinekens in the minibar. Not that we've ever used hotel minibars, but their presence is nice. It was the most comfortable hotel we had stayed in for the whole trip—probably for my whole life. At almost 2:00 a.m., we finally settled in to our clean, comfortable beds. Unfortunately, to our ignorance, the next day was Easter, and prices soared. We decided to find another place to stay. After searching and asking, we wound up staying in an illegal business that sold rooms by the night in public housing project apartments. It was small, dirty, and uncomfortable, plus it smelled bad—but at least it had a window to the ocean. And it was only $200 MOD. Plus the location was good, and there was a bed and bathroom, and, really, nothing else was necessary.

The next day, we rode buses all around town, trying to find more interesting spots. After a few uninteresting temples and gardens, we made it to Mr. Lu's mansion, a large house from the end of the Qing Dynasty, about 120 years ago. Although there were no signs or information brochures, there were guided tours in Portuguese and English every hour. But we didn't want to wait another hour, so we asked some of the workers why the house was so special that it was made into a historical landmark, and a very nice Macanese boy offered to give us a free tour in English. Suddenly, the boring old house became interesting. There was symbology hidden in the walls, the floors, and the decorations, making me realize that one should not judge a book by its cover.

Sometimes even the most plain-appearing person or object can turn out to be fascinating—it just takes the right person to get the most out of them. For example, a regular person may see a rock on the ground and kick it away, while a trained archaeologist may recognize it as a rare fossil or a new discovery. Therefore, if we judge a book by only its cover, you may miss a great treasure.

HELLO AGAIN, CHINA

By afternoon, we were officially in the Republic of China. The change was instantly noticeable. Everything was dirtier and older, and there were fake PSPs and iPhones, as well as every other purchasable item, on sale and in use everywhere. A uniformed man at a portable stand motioned to us and offered to arrange a hotel. Although you would think that a man in a uniform with a portable stand doing business next to multiple security officers would be trustworthy, that is not always the case in mainland China. "Newly built," he said. "Elegant twin suite," he claimed. "Only a few minutes from here," he promised. When we got there, we found that it was a very old, small hotel, dark and musty, moldy-smelling, with cigarette burns and gum all over the carpet. Also, it was a $ 16 RMB taxi ride from the terminal, almost twice his claim that it would be under $ 10 RMB. I guess Macao's experience did not apply here. We vowed not to trust any Chinese businessmen again unless we could see what we were getting first.

The city through which we reentered into China is called Zhuhai, and it had the most busy customs entrance we had ever seen. It seemed to have not too many tourists, but many local people were doing business; they carried cheap local Chinese produce to Macao and carried some fancy products to China for those people who were eager for new technology.

It was interesting to see how the local people made a living. We joined one local tour to sightsee. But there was not much to see, so by noon we headed to another big booming city in southern China, Shenzhen. After a few hours on the bus, we were in Shenzhen. A modern, huge, and still-developing new city, its face is very different from Zhuhai. The bus drove us through the city, and we were surprised by its sleek, modern look. We were overwhelmed by the size and pace of this strange city, totally lost, and had no clue how to find a hotel that fit our budget. In the end, being tired of dragging around our luggage searching for a room for the night, we decided to stay in an okay-looking hotel near the bus station but found it pretty crappy after we checked in.

In 2010, Tomb-Sweeping Day was April 5. It is a major Chinese holiday when people go to their ancestors' graves to pay respects and maintain them in good condition. If they are not near any of their ancestors' graves, they typically go to local temples to pay respect, burn incense, and pray in honor of their ancestors. In Taiwan, Tomb-Sweeping Day is no longer a single day but just any day soon after Lantern Festival, the last day of the Chinese New Year celebration. This was delegated to help reduce traffic jams and crowding at temples. However, in mainland China, it is still a national holiday and there is vacation from school and work, and when we got to Xianhu (Fairy Lake) Park, it was completely filled—a perfect example of the Chinese idiom "mountains and oceans of people." There were cars lining up on every road around the mountain, and at least hundreds of thousands of people walking up and down the mountain to Hongfa Temple to pay respects. The traffic was so bad that walking was actually faster, although much more tiring and less comfortable. Despite some inconvenience, seeing so many people come so far to pay respects to their ancestors and deities was heartwarming and gave us hope for the future of Chinese culture and tradition.

TRUE COURAGE

It was my job to take care of the money for the whole trip. I felt I was doing a good job, but I had still made a few mistakes—forgetting twenty dollars here, fifty dollars there—and in the end, my records were more than three hundred dollars off. As my mom reprimanded me, I felt myself getting angry again. It was only a few U.S. dollars! Why was she yelling at me again? I started having a bad attitude and tried to avoid the subject, but I could not deny that I had made some mistakes and the records did not match the money. Of course, my frustration did not help, and things escalated until we were both yelling at each other. In the end, I realized that my mom was not criticizing me but simply trying to help me to understand myself and improve myself—if I had a problem I should take the comment in stride, be honest and face the mistake, learn from it and do better next time.

According to the teachings of Confucius, bravery is not measured in medals of war or battle scars, body counts or enemies slain. True bravery is conquering oneself and taking responsibility for one's own actions, especially mistakes. If one hides his own wrongdoings, then how can he improve himself? Hiding the mistake only doubles the sin, while admitting it and finding a solution fixes it and shows true courage. As I reflected shamefully upon my dishonorable, unfilial actions, I thought of Dao Zhen from Jushiling. He would never hide his mistakes, and never argued with others; he only focused on finding solutions to the problems, whether they were his fault or not.

PART VI

ENLIGHTENMENT

April ~ May 2010

THE YOUNGEST ENLIGHTENED
HUMAN BEING

On that happy note, we departed Shenzhen for Guangzhou, in search of sites related to the Sixth Patriarch of Zen Buddhism, Master Hui Neng.

Master Hui Neng (638–713 AD) was a monk from the Tang Dynasty (618–907 AD). He is famous for being the youngest human known to have been enlightened, at twenty-four years old, even younger than Siddhartha Guatemala, also known as Sakyamuni Buddha, or just "The Buddha," was. His father died at a young age, and as a child, he had to chop and sell firewood to support his mother and himself. One day, outside of a guesthouse, he heard a scholar reading the Diamond Sutra, and was enthralled. "What are you reading?" he asked the scholar enthusiastically. The scholar introduced the Diamond Sutra and teachings of Buddhism to Hui Neng, who immediately interpreted it with the clarity of a skilled monk. The scholar was greatly impressed and encouraged him to learn from the Fifth Patriarch of Zen Buddhism, Master Hong Ren, in Huangmei Mountain.

"But I still have to work to support my elderly mother," Hui Neng said dejectedly. However, he did not have to worry, as the scholar knew that he was in the presence of an exceptional man, and that he should do anything in his power to support him. As soon as he heard Hui Neng's words, the scholar gave him a large sum of money—enough to support his mother for the rest of her life—and Hui Neng set off in search of enlightenment.

Upon arriving at the Zen temple of the Fifth Patriarch, he begged the Patriarch to let him become a monk. However, the Patriarch appeared to ridicule him, saying, "You? A Cantonese southerner? You are a barbarian! Why do you come to this temple?"

Hui Neng, undeterred, promptly replied, "I come only in search of Buddhahood."

The Fifth Patriarch, impressed by his resolve, sent him to work in the kitchen chopping firewood and washing rice. After eight months, the Patriarch saw that Hui Neng was no mundane person—he was ready to inherit the legendary bowl and robe, and become the Sixth Patriarch of Zen Buddhism. However, as he was only twenty-four years old, and not even a monk, the Patriarch knew that it was not yet safe. Therefore, he secretly transferred the bowl and robe into Hui Neng's hands at a midnight meeting, and advised him to hide until he knew it was safe.

Hui Neng ran from the temple and headed south, and as soon as the other monks knew, they chased furiously after him, intending to take back the bowl and robe and to kill Hui Neng. However, not one of them was successful. With his infinite wisdom, he was able to influence and touch an uncountable number of beings. His teachings and story continue to move people today, with many of the temples and towns he once walked in remain in tribute to him.

THE WIND, THE FLAG, OR THE HEART?

The first site we visited was Guangxiao Temple, in Guangzhou. The legend is that after fifteen years in hiding, Hui Neng turned up at this temple, and was listening to the abbot give a Buddhist lecture, when two monks started debating.

"It is the flag that is moving," said one. "No," the other argued. "It is the wind that is moving."

Hui Neng stepped up, and proclaimed, "Neither the flag nor the wind are moving. It is your hearts that are moving."

Personally, I would just say that both the flag and the wind are moving...but Buddhism always goes deeper than just physical descriptions. Hui Neng was hinting at the transparency and illusions of this world, the concept that everything we see is a direct product of the thoughts and projections of our own hearts.

Impressed by Hui Neng's wisdom, the abbot of the temple stepped up and questioned whether Hui Neng was the legendary Sixth Patriarch. Hui Neng, knowing that the time was right, acknowledged his status and was finally officially ordained as a monk, having his head shaved. After shaving Hui Neng's head, the abbot of the temple turned around and bowed to Hui Neng, imploring him to accept him as a student. The abbot's astounding humbleness, not polluted by jealousy at all, had surprised everyone; even the Buddhist practitioners of today are awestruck. But Hui Neng was even more humble, and said, "The monk that shaved my head is my teacher, and technically cannot be my student!" But after the abbot insisted, Hui Neng agreed to let them both look up to and recognize the Fifth Patriarch as their teacher. The abbot's high recognition had helped Master Hui Neng start his teaching rapidly, and his humble attitude had also earned himself a great reputation. These two great men have set a most auspicious example for their followers and touched Chinese people's hearts for over a thousand years, and the teachings from Master Hui Neng have had immense influence in Chinese and Buddhist history. More than a thousand years later, his story and teachings are still widely spread among Buddhists the world over.

As I strolled around the temple, reading the story that he had left in Guagxiao temple, I contemplated the ordination ceremony that was said to be the biggest event at that time, drawing all the famous monks to join this great moment. How spectacular it would have been! Although I could not go back to join them, being able to stand here in the exact same temple that the history was written made me feel like I was bathing under the Buddha light.

The temple also had a Bodhi tree that was planted by an Indian monk who came to China to visit, the first Bodhi tree ever planted in China. It is said that every Bodhi tree in China today is a descendant of the one at Guangxiao Temple. On his visit to Guangxiao Temple, this Indian monk also prophesied that, around seven hundred years later, a "living Buddha" would be ordained as a monk at this very temple. In addition, Guangxiao Temple's main hall is the oldest structure in southern China, and besides Hui Neng, the first Patriarch of Zen Buddhism, the famous Indian monk, Damo, also practiced here.

FINDING HIS BIRTH PLACE

Although Hui Neng is extremely famous among Buddhists, most people in China do not know much about him, and so our pilgrimage to his hometown was not very easy. We were told that to get there we would have to take a bus from Guangzhou to Yunfu, about three hours, then take another bus to Xinxing, another hour and a half, then another bus to Liuzhu village, about half an hour. Then, to get to the next temple, we would have to go all the way back to Guangzhou and take a bus to that town, Shaoguan. However, once we got to Xinxing, we were surprised to learn that it had buses directly from Guangzhou. We had wasted more than $50 RMB in money for bus tickets, and a one-night hotel stay on the way.

Upon arriving at the site of Master Hui Neng's home, where a shrine to him now stands, I felt a rush of gratefulness and wonder. My mom, being even more sincere, immediately started crying and bowing emotionally. How many people have the fortune to stand before such a great man's birthplace? How many Christians have walked in the footsteps of Jesus Christ? How many have paid respects to Martin Luther King, Jr., or Henry Ford, or Isaac Newton, at their hometown or grave or any other historic site so closely related to them? We saw the property on which he grew up, the town in which he lived before becoming a monk, and a Lychee tree that he planted himself, more than 1,300 years ago.

According to legend, this Lychee tree only flowers and grows fruit when the country of China is in a good state. During Sun Yat-Sen's just revolution against the Qing Dynasty to benefit the people of China, the tree was flowering; but during the Cultural Revolution, which did irreparable damage and destruction to countless families and ancient Chinese cultures, the tree looked almost dead. This year, in the midst of China's economic rise on the world stage, the tree is flowering robustly again. Due to these inexplicable coincidences, this tree is also known as the "Nation's Luck Tree."

FACE TO FACE WITH
MASTER HUI NENG

After a few days relaxing in Hui Neng's hometown, we headed far, far away to the town of Shaoguan, where his holy remains are located. Preserved for 1,300 years, his body is a physical sign of the purity of his heart. After all, preservatives did not exist 1,300 years ago, and the Chinese culture did not include making mummies. The 95 percent humidity of Guangdong also left no chance of creating natural mummies, a fact demonstrated by the conspicuous paucity of mummies from the area. It is believed that Master Hui Neng had simply attained a level of enlightenment where he could detach his mind from his body, and when he left his body, it remained as it has been for 1,300 years. It still looks to be in its original condition.

There is a story that, during the Cultural Revolution, a skeptic did not believe that it was his actual body, and cut open his chest to reveal internal organs. Upon seeing all the organs perfectly in place and detailed, he was so shocked and awestruck that he immediately bowed down in respect.

As we entered the temple, we knew that at last we would see Hui Neng's real body. At the highest altar room in the temple rested Hui Neng's real body. It was dark, shining gold, but largely obscured by the glare of its glass case. It looked as if it could be made of solid gold, but the proportions and shapes were identical to those of a real human's. I gazed at his holy remains and tried to convince myself we finally were face to face with the youngest enlightened human. It was hard to believe that his body had sat there like a monk in deep meditation for almost 1,300 years. My mom bowed immediately and wished that she could bow there forever and never leave, but there were so many other people waiting behind us to pay their respects that we had to leave quickly so that they could have their turns.

The temple is big, containing many halls which were constructed on a slope. In one particular hall there were many historical items exhibited, including many gifts and letters from the emperor of the Tang Dynasty, Wu ZheTien, the only female emperor in Chinese history. She had invited Master Hui Neng to the palace and asked him to be the teacher of the country, and of course the teacher of the emperor herself. But Master Hui Neng gently turned down the offer and remained teaching in the south, where his home province was located. We were also told that the famous "robe and bowl" are also safely kept in this building, but only can be seen by some very special people. Approval is required by the local officer as well as the abbot of this temple to show this historic "robe and bowl."

Feeling this holy atmosphere, we lingered about the whole temple, trying to purify our minds. We were fortunate enough to find an afternoon praying class, and we joined the monks in their prayers. After praying, we went to have dinner in the temple with the volunteers, and then headed back to see Master Hui Neng again. By this time, it was much quieter and many of the visitors had left. Coming once again into the shrine where his body sat, we knelt and bowed a hundred times, knowing that few people were lucky enough to have this opportunity and that we were truly blessed. Unfortunately, the shrine was closing soon, so we had to leave again. As I took a last look through the shrine's doors at Master Hui Neng's silhouette, I was reminded, again, of how lucky I really was and how few people ever had opportunities like this. Unwilling to leave, we were hoping to absorb the essence of his spirit and enjoyed the atmosphere of being in Hui Neng's presence, and were the last visitors to leave. Despite the steady drizzle and gray sky, everything seemed to glow, and the large expanse of marble in front of the temple reflected everything on top of it like a vast glass surface. The effect was magical.

The highest altar room in Nanhua Zen Temple where Master Hui Neng's physical body is resting. Pictures are not allowed to be taken directly of his body.

THE FAMOUS
"DISASTER HIDING ROCK"

By that night, it had started raining rather heavily, and by the next morning, it was still showering. All of the dirt had turned into deep, slippery mud, and the roads were covered in it. A few steps outside resulted in wet feet, and there were puddles everywhere. Despite this, it was our last day in this village, and my mom was determined not to leave before seeing the famous "disaster-hiding rock," where Hui Neng had hidden from the other monks who were after his bowl and robe, who had set fire to the whole mountain. The legend goes that Hui Neng, seeing the fire, jumped up and, using powers beyond the normal human's abilities, sealed himself inside of the rock, thus finding a sanctuary which ended up being the only spot on the entire mountain that wasn't scorched.

That morning, we went again to the temple and inquired about the rock. They told us that it was right across the street, but it was miles down a long, muddy road and up an also long, significantly muddier and undrivable hill. I kept complaining and tried to convince my mother it wasn't worth it. My mom could not pass up this opportunity, ignored me, and quickly found a local to drive us to the base of the hill. Upon arrival, we were unpleasantly surprised by the hill being even muddier than we had originally envisioned. I thought my mom would have given up after seeing the muddy mountain road, especially since the rain had started falling heavier and heavier. To my surprise, my mother rolled up her pants, marched into that mud, climbed up the hill, and left me no choice but to follow her.

For the whole trip, not another soul was to be seen. We carefully hiked up, eventually made it to the top of the hill, and saw the rock. It was magnificent and towered twenty feet above its surroundings, with a suspicious hole in the middle that was almost the perfect size for a human to sit in. It was interesting, to say the least. A miracle? Maybe. But maybe not. Maybe it was just a big dent in a giant boulder. Either way, it was something that most people do not get to see, and as we started back down the slippery, slippery slope, I felt a surge of appreciation.

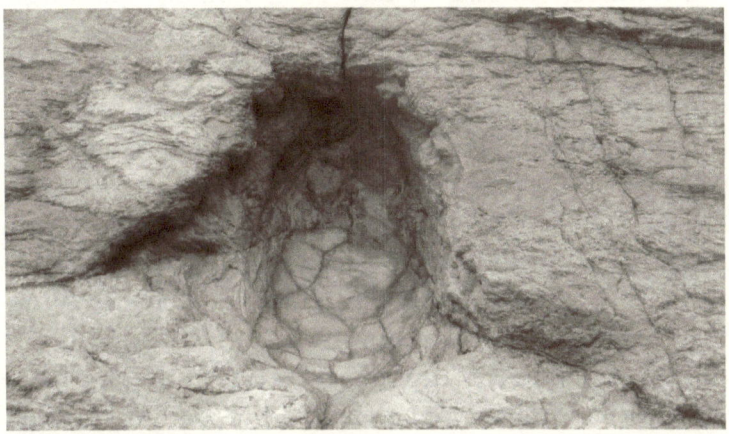

The Famous Disaster Hiding Rock, where Master Hui Neng, seeing the fire that was set by the monks who tried to kill him, jumped up and, using powers beyond the normal human's abilities, sealed himself inside of the rock. The hole was almost the perfect size for a human to fit in.

AN EXTREME TRAIL

During our pilgrimage tour of Master Hui Neng, we made a small detour to Danxia Mountain, which was in the vicinity of Shaoguan. Although not too famous outside of China, everybody in the region urged us to see it, claiming that it was beautiful and we should not miss it. Having already seen Yellow Mountain, we doubted that there could be any mountain more magnificent, but since every mountain was unique, we decided to visit.

Danxia Mountain ended up being the most "extreme" mountain we had ever climbed—although most of the trails were tame and normal, *nothing* compared to the floating section of trail on a newly developed part of Yellow Mountain, there was one trail on Danxia Mountain that was like nothing we had ever seen before. It started off steep and did not get any easier. The first length was almost like a ladder, with metal steps jutting up at perhaps a 75-degree angle. After we had passed that particular obstacle, we came face to face with not so much a path as huge boulders that had had footholds carved into them, which we had to climb up at near 90-degrees, with other rocks behind us and, besides some chains staked into the rock, few safety features. Two of the three other groups of people we encountered were too scared to continue.

We climbed all the way to the gazebo on the peak. It was the most extreme trail we had experienced.

After about three of these boulders and impassably narrow sections of path, we made it to the top, feeling victorious, and thankfully, there was another path to go down, although as we found out, this one was also rather steep, with long lengths that were on a slope of perhaps 75 degrees.

The next day, we went on the bigger, easier paths, which passed by many Buddhist and Daoist temples. One temple in particular was special—it was built directly into the cliffs on the side of the mountain, with hard mountain rock serving as the back wall. Also, in stark contrast to many of the temples we had seen, especially in tourist spots, the nuns there were very warm and welcoming, inviting us to stay with them and teaching us about Buddhism. The ones who did not talk to us all seemed to be very diligently practicing. Even more amazing, not one of them asked for money or donations like many other places in China, a fact that just compelled us to donate more to them in support of their attitude and practice. From one free-book stand and TV room, we found out that they also learned from Master Chin Kung's books and DVDs, the same source of our Buddhist education.

BIG PICTURE & SMALL DOT

After exploring Danxia Mountain, we headed to a small town to see another historical site of Master Hui Neng. Unfortunately, my mom was sick, and I was trying as hard as I could to take good care of her. I was running around the whole neighborhood near the hotel in this strange new town in which we just arrived, looking for medicine and fresh fruits to buy for her. So when she said she was hungry, I tried just as hard to find dinner, made more difficult by the fact that we are vegetarian and the odd vacuum devoid of food stores or restaurants near our hotel.

I ended up walking more than two kilometers, and after one hour, I decided to turn back and report that I could not find any vegetarian food. On the way back, I walked on the opposite side of the road, asked every restaurant I passed. Finally, I had found one who said they could make vegetarian fried rice and tofu. Right after I ordered, my mom called me. I had been gone for an hour and twenty minutes, and the sky had already been dark for more than half an hour. Understandably, she was worried. I apologized and, after getting the food, ran back to the hotel, outpacing all of the tuk-tuks and pedestrians.

After getting back to the hotel, I realized how worried my mother had been, that she had only expected me to be gone for a few minutes and go a few blocks, not nearly two hours and four kilometers. A job that should only take a few minutes should not take much longer unless there is something wrong, and if something goes wrong, people should be notified so that there is no misunderstanding or worrying. Through some arguing, I finally realized that I have been in a habit of focusing on one thing and forgetting everything else since I was little.

Often I do not see the big picture but a small dot of it. Just as my mom always tells me, "You can't see the forest for the trees." After almost one year when I am typing this, I am able to imagine my mom's perspective: in a remote strange city of a foreign country, it is scary to depart with your child for so long with such a simple mission.

ROBE-BOWL ROCK

The next day, we went to Robe-Bowl Rock, the rock where Hui Neng supposedly set his robe and alms bowl down. When the first monk of the group that was chasing him tried to take them back, he could not even lift them a bit. The monk immediately knew Hui Neng was not mundane and bowed down to him and asked for a lesson. Hui Neng asked him a few very wise questions, which made the monk, reach some level of enlightenment right away. This is a very famous legend which has been past down generation by generation, and still one of the most popular stories in Hui Neng's life.

It was another long, tedious bus ride away, near the border of Guangdong and Jiangxi provinces. I had become a little bit sick and had a headache, so I really did not want to go, but my mom convinced me that it would be a waste of time to stay in bed and rest all day. Robe-Bowl Rock was on Meiguan Ancient Path, an ancient pathway built by hand to make travel easier. It was one of the first of its kind, using precisely cut stones to make a relatively smooth, flat, durable surface. And more than 1,300 years later, it still retains its original charm and beauty and is still in good condition.

Throughout the hike, my headache only got worse, but I still let my mom convince me to hike the whole length. When we got to the top, the view was amazing. We could see both provinces, along with two rivers intersecting. It had been raining earlier in the day, and there were puddles everywhere, one of which had a beetle drowning in it. As soon as I saw the beetle, I swooped down to pick it up and let it fly away, but it kept coming back to me, so I took pictures with it. I felt that the beetle was staying with me to show its gratitude for saving its life.

After resting for a few minutes at the top, we slowly began the long climb down. The stairs were still wet and slippery, but we managed to make it down without incident. On the way down, I still had a headache, so we stopped next to Robe-Bowl Rock and I rested there for almost an hour. My mom thought I was deep in thought, but really, I was just watching the raindrops fall into a puddle and wondering when the puddle would overflow. My only emotions were exhaustion and anticipation—anticipation of when my headache would be over, when I would go back home and to school, when my dad would get here and we would start going to tourist sites instead of Buddhist spots and having fun.

Looking back, however, I am amazed by Hui Neng's story, and I have come to the realization of just how precious it was that I was able to go down the actual path he walked and touch what is claimed as the actual rock that his robe and bowl were on.

Robe-Bowl Rock, where Master Hui Neng put down his Robe and Bowl which could not be moved. It is located on the ancient Meiguan path, on the border of Guangdong and Jiangxi province.

PART VII

HEAD WEST, OLD MAN

May 2010

A MOTHER'S LOVE

After getting back from Robe-Bowl Rock, we made our way back to Shaoguan, getting off the bus at the train station. I was still sick, so instead of moving on to the next city, we decided to take some time to relax, and we got a room in one of the nicer hotels there, a three-star hotel with a nice view of the river and city. It was the second-nicest room we had stayed in all year, with a wide-open space, a flat-screen TV, and two large, clean, comfortable beds. The view out of the window was great, and that night, the city lights lit up the whole window. It had been a long time since I had seen a city landscape like that.

As I lay in bed all day, my mom ran around buying fresh fruit for me and taking care of me—massaging me, giving me water, tea, and food, and praying for me. She did a better job than my care for her when she was sick, even though she was not completely recovered from her illness. I could really see how much she loved and cared for me. At the end of the day, we were both exhausted and fell into a deep sleep. The next morning, my headache was gone, so we began to seek out the way to Guilin. It had begun to rain heavily that night, and it was still raining that day, but according to the train schedule, the earliest train was at 4:00 p.m. The checkout time was 12:00 noon, so we left our luggage at the front desk and went across the river into Shaoguan's downtown and walked the streets. It was an interesting city, with some nice parks and modern art installments, and we had a good time, even though it was raining. When 4:00 came, we finally got back to the train station, once again exhausted.

A FLIP REACTION AND
A UNIQUE SCENE

I hated when my mom asked me to do stuff by myself. It made me feel like she didn't believe I could do it, and I don't know why she would make me buy stuff or order food while she just watched. So when she asked me to buy our train tickets from Shaoguan to Guilin, I had another flip reaction, refusing to buy them and accusing her of degrading me.

After almost an hour of discussion and argument, I realized that my mom simply wanted me to practice skills that I would use in everyday life, and be more confident in my dealings with the rest of the world. She kept reminding me that I should do things not to prove I can do them, and not to satisfy my parents, but because it is the right thing to do and to nurture them to become a good habit. It was for my own benefit, she claimed. I did not agree with her at that time, but now after I have read Di Zi Gui for more than a year, I refer the incident to Confucius teaching, I think it is a child's honor and responsibility to serve the elder, especially their parents and teachers. I felt a sense of guilt that I had never made things easy for my mother and she had to go through so many hard times similar to this. I also deeply appreciate her patience to try so hard to let me understand such a simple concept.

The train ride to Guilin in Guangxi was once again a long tiring trip—23.5 hours, to be exact. We opted for the twice-as-expensive "hard sleeper," where only the top bunks were still available, which, as we found out, had approximately two feet of headroom. Although it was a mild nuisance and inconvenience, I was unperturbed and, within a few hours, had settled down to sleep.

My mother, on the other hand, complained about it long enough that another passenger, who had a middle bunk, offered to switch with her. I rolled my eyes and fell asleep. At about 3:30 a.m., I suddenly woke up, rolled off the end of my bed, grabbed the rungs of the ladder, and lowered myself silently into my Nikes. Besides a man in his fifties sitting on a chair and gazing through the window, nobody appeared to be awake.

After the requisite bathroom trip, I too sat on a chair, shrouding myself in the curtain so that I could see out of the window. I watched small, empty train stations whisk by, night watchmen shining their flashlights at us, and saw the soft shimmer of moonlight reflecting off of the surface of water in terraced fields. Neither of us spoke. At about 5:30, I climbed back into my bed and did not wake up again until we were almost at our destination.

Once we got to Guilin, we immediately took the next bus to Yangzhuo, which was only a few hours' bus ride away. Upon arrival, it was immediately obvious that we were in a tourist town. White people were everywhere, and although school was in session, at least in the northern hemisphere, there was an abundance of people from seemingly every country. Rented bicycles flooded the streets, and 95 percent of the storefronts seemed to be hotels, souvenir shops, bars, restaurants, and cafes. Upon closer examination, it was easy to see why the area had attracted so many tourists.

The scenery was so unique and unparalleled that it was used as the background for one of the alien planets in Star Wars movies. What makes Guilin and Yangzhou so famous is their abundance of steep, sudden mountains, which occurred naturally and form a truly unique landscape of cliffs and jagged stones jutting up from seemingly nowhere. In addition to these unique mountains, there is a network of rivers running in and around them, making for a truly unparalleled sight. The rivers reflect the mountains and create balance and symmetry in the scenery, and the pine trees growing on the bare rock add to the magic.

ONE MONTH WITH DAD

After a few days of staying in Yangzhuo by ourselves, and the long, eventually successful search for a good hotel that fit our budget, we went to pick up my dad, who had again flown out to us from America and would be spending the next month in China with us. Seeing him again for the first time in China and second time in the year, I was very happy. I actually missed him a lot, and I almost could not believe that he was here, with us, in mainland China, for the next month. It was almost surreal, too good to be true. In the past few months, we had seen so many spectacular sights and gone to so many sacred sites, but one special person was always missing: my dad. Without my dad there, all of the experiences seemed empty. We wished he could have been there with us the whole time and seen everything, but he had to work. Even though he was not with us, we thought of him all the time and planned our whole trip around him, considering when and where to meet him so that he would see the best places and waste the least amount of time possible.

The relaxed and laid-back atmosphere of Yangzhuo was a welcome change from the previous cities we had visited, bustling and busy. It was also a great relaxing resort for my Dad from his daily routine. On any night in Yangzhuo, there was something to do: we were browsing the interesting streets, exploring tourist shops and restaurants, and we seemed to never get bored. In the daytime, we rented bicycles, biked the country roads to nearby parks, and hiked. We once biked up and down the river and came across small villages and shops, going along paths that were almost completely devoid of tourists. A family with small children in shoulder baskets blocked off our path and charged us for taking pictures of them. At a nice little shop, my dad had a beer while my mom talked with a local, an ex-army man who had a variety of strange hats, including one that he made out of a few sticks and leaves from a bush while we were resting. We saw buffalo and fields, and one farmer working in his field got angry when he saw us and demanded that we let him see our camera so he could delete any pictures of him. We biked on and left him behind. The roads were still muddy in many places, and my Air Max 2s, which I had managed to keep relatively clean so far, finally had to get dirty.

At night, the whole city lit up. There were karaoke bars, nightclubs, restaurants, and of course shops. The atmosphere was nice, not too busy or loud, but far from boring. We went to a restaurant and watched a free movie there every night.

We also went to famous caves near Yangzhuo, including the "Silver Cave." The caves we saw were beautiful and amazing, but we felt that the neon lights bathing them in a Technicolor glow took away from their beauty. The stalactites and stalagmites were amazing, stretching tens of feet from the floor to the ceiling, but the red, green, and blue lights bathing the whole cave made it look more artificial than natural. In fact, the effect was so overpowering that we constantly had to remind ourselves that the formations were natural and not made of concrete. All the same, the caves were amazing, and I enjoyed observing the various unique formations with my dad, including ones that looked like a miniature Great Wall of China and stalactites that stretched more than forty feet, inches away from touching the ground, and speculating how they had formed.

On another day, we cruised down the Li River, the main river that ran the long distance through the cities of Guilin and Yangzhou. It is the Li River which is so famous and in so many pictures, reflecting the unique mountains of Guilin that made this place one of the most famous tourist spots in the world, and it had been the main thoroughfare for the area. We took a bus a few miles upriver and paid a man on a small bamboo boat with a motor attached to float us back down, stopping along the way at key points. One of the views was on the twenty-dollar bill of Chinese money. I would have preferred a boat without a motor, but it was enjoyable nonetheless, and the four hours floating on the Li River was an unforgettably beautiful experience.

HELLO, DALI

After Yangzshuo, we took another train for about twenty hours to Kunming, in Yunnan province. Kunming is the capital of Yunnan, and is a very large city. We were there during the weekdays, but as usual, there were an astounding number of people on the streets, even during working hours. After settling on the hotel, we went over to a large nearby City Park during the daytime and were stunned by the number of people. Even though it was 2:00 p.m. on a weekday, the park had so many people that it was hard not to bump into anyone. Besides the people, there was also an area full of street performers. People dressed in costumes played mandolins, sang, and danced in the traditional ethnic fashion, representing different ethnic minorities' customs. There were also people selling all sort of different fresh fruit on the street, which was pretty common in Chinese cities. We bought a peeled pineapple on a stick, and it was a relief on the hot day and also much healthier than the street food such as ice cream or sodas that people have in America. Sadly, we could not stay in Kunming too long because of my dad's limited time and so many places that we planned to visit with him, so the next day, we set off for Dali.

Dali, another charming tourist city, was another long train ride away. Since it was some holiday again, all of the trains were full, so the one we took was actually added to the regular train schedule. After two experiences of the uncomfortable sleeping bed ticket, this time we bought seat tickets. Surprisingly, the whole train was all bunk beds: each six-bed compartment had about twelve people in it, and the train workers actually went up and down the train, checking and prohibiting people from lying down. Although most of the cars near us were full, there were actually two or three at the end that were almost completely empty. As I was in the habit of pacing aimlessly up and down cars, hoping somebody would talk to me, I was one of the few that knew about these empty cars, and I lay down to sleep in one when the train workers had stopped caring.

Dali was completely different from Yangzhuo. Its streets were wider and emptier, and the downtown area seemed to be smaller. The old town was a small section of Dali which was enclosed by an ancient city wall. It was only really active in one half, which was full of bars and shops that were open all night, while the other half was more residential and quiet. My parents and I enjoyed walking around the old town, exploring its streets, which included one "Foreigner Street" full of more Western-friendly stores, and eating the street food, including Yunnan's famous green bean noodles and fried yak cheese painted with rose paste, locally known as "cheese fans."

After finding a hotel and seeing Dali's old town and Erhai Lake, along with a few other nearby attractions, we set off to Jizu Mountain, more than four hours and two buses away from downtown Dali, which was one half-hour public bus away from the old town where we stayed.

A LIVE MODEL OF CAUSE AND EFFECT

Jizu Mountain is a lesser-known scenic attraction, which is also an important site for Buddhists. On the first bus heading to our destination, my parents, as usual, began talking to passengers, two college students who were sitting next to them. After the bus ride together, we stayed with the college students, Vicky and Marth, eating lunch together, and I hiked up the mountain with them while my parents took the cable car. Normally, there were very few tourists on the mountain, but today was May 1, Labor Day, and a lot of people were going to the mountain to see the sunrise and temples. During the hike up, I started talking to them more and became more comfortable with them. I like making friends, but I am usually just too scared to talk to people I don't know. However, through my parents getting to know them, I became friends with them too.

By the time we had gotten to the top of the mountain, my parents had befriended a middle-aged man, Mr. Yan. My parents found out that he was a businessman in Kunming, in the construction industry, and had gotten to where he was today from having nothing.

More than five years earlier, he had attempted to open his own small business in Kunming after he was retired from the military, but it had failed and all his investments were lost. Homeless, jobless, and starving, his wife left him. Depressed and broke, he lived on the streets of Kunming for months, until one day he met an old Buddhist monk. The monk taught him about the principles of Cause and Effect, and advised him to selflessly and enthusiastically do good deeds. From that day on, he did as much as he could to help others. Although broke, he was still in good shape from his former army training, and, at just shy of forty years old, still in decent physical shape. Therefore, he would help people carry bags, do work, anything he could to make other people's lives easier. The principle seemed to be true, because within a few years, he had gone from starving and broke to having his own company, a car, a house, and an overflowing income, which allowed him to donate money to charities and needy people. According to Mr. Yan, he donated $ 10,000 RMB to the victims of the Qinghai earthquake alone. He has become one of the happiest and richest men in the world because he has made so many friends through helping others.

His first wife came back looking for him after he had gotten his life back in order. He had already remarried. Although he was loud and rough, his enthusiasm to help others and learn about Buddhism still made him a good role model, and he had vowed to go to Buddhist temples to learn whenever he could— the reason that he was at Jizu Mountain. His attitude has inspired me. Now, when I see people carrying heavy things or having trouble in public, I do whatever I can to help them solve their problems. Helping people is good for the soul, and you can almost always expect at least a smile and a happy "thank you." And more importantly, those good deeds acting as a cause will lead to a good effect, just as the farmers' seeds will germinate a harvest.

THREE COURSES OF TEA

The next day, we got up early, ate another bowl of the famous local Yunnan noodles, made from green beans and served cold with sauce, for breakfast, and set off on our journey with the driver we hired for the day.

Our first stop was a boat cruise around the Erhai, the lake right next to Dali that is so big it is more commonly referred to as an "inland sea." In fact, the opposite side is too far away to be seen, so it really does have the appearance of a sea. The boat cruise was run by the Bai People, another ethnic group that was prominent near Dali, and during the cruise, between destinations, we learned some of their culture.

Most memorable was the Bai People's "three courses of tea," a tradition that the Bai people have passed down for centuries. The three courses of tea are three different kinds of tea, served in a special sequence as part of a customary ceremony used, among other things, for welcoming guests. The first tea is bitter, the second one is sweet, and the third is herbal and minty, which they called "aftertaste tea." The bitter tea was too bitter and not good, and the sweet tea was too sweet, like drinking sugar water, so I did not like either of them, but the third tea was very special, with a unique minty flavor which lingered in the mouth, and was my favorite of the three. The three courses of tea reflect the three phases of life: the bitter hard work that must be endured during one's youth, the sweet reward once the hard work is finished, and the everlasting memories once everything else has been experienced.

It is a very interesting and different philosophy than Western culture. I always thought my mom is the only crazy person in the world who loves bitter food such as bitter melon and ginger tea, which I hate the most. It had been always a puzzle for me, but now with the Bai people's three courses of tea, I finally caught a glimpse of this strange philosophy.

A MOMENT OF PANIC

After the cruise, we met our driver and drove around some more to other destinations. We saw some interesting caves and mountains, but the other big highlight of the day was when the driver drove off with all our backpacks, which contained all of our money, cell phone, passports, and records of the trip. We had asked to stop and take a picture at the famous Three Pagodas, and in less than five minutes after we took our pictures, our car was nowhere to be seen. In a panic, we walked around the whole sight looking for the car. Confused and disbelieving, my dad found our hotel's card in his pocket, we borrowed somebody's cell phone to call the manager, who had booked our driver, exclaiming that our backpacks including passports had been taken away by the driver.

We thought that we were completely screwed. Without passports, how could we make it back home? What would they do with our passports? With no money or credit cards or ID, how would we ever even get out of Dali? Almost half an hour had passed, and we still did not see our car. However, there was one car parked on the side of the road that looked kind of like ours...but it had a different driver and was on a different road, so we did not bother checking it further.

Finally, after ten more minutes, we decided to ask the driver if she had seen our driver, and then we realized that this was our car, just with a different driver.

The woman, who had received a phone call from the hotel manager, explained that it had all been a misunderstanding; her husband had to go to another customer beyond their plan, so they had to switch cars. Apparently, he did not get a chance to tell us, causing us half an hour's panic. The lesson we learned was to never leave personal belongings, especially important things like money and documents, behind when you are traveling, even if you think you can trust the person.

THE CHANGING FACE
OF CHINA

Our next spot was Lijiang, another whole day's ride in a small bus through miles of twisty mountain roads. It was touted as one of the most beautiful and peaceful places in China, but when we arrived, we found the exact opposite. Although still beautiful, it was nowhere near what we had heard; the recent drought had left huge swaths of the greenery yellowed and dry, and the downtown area itself had even more bars and nightclubs than Yangzhuo and Dali combined.

Witnessing this changing face of China, my mom was happy that we made the decision to visit southwest China instead of the developed north; for every year this once remote and exotic minor ethnic culture will gradually disappear because of the pouring in of tourism, yet the developed north will retain the same face for years, and will be waiting for us to explore.

Once we had arrived in Lijiang, we had to take a taxi to the old town section. My dad had befriended an elderly Australian lady and her daughter on the bus ride, neither of whom could speak Chinese, so we offered to help them find their hotel. We boarded one of the van-taxis waiting for business outside of the bus station and started trying to communicate with the driver. Unfortunately, the driver was a local man who had grown up speaking the local dialect and had a strong accent when speaking Mandarin. Even my mother could not understand anything he said. He kept talking excitedly and gesturing wildly, but my mom could not make any sense of it. Both of them were getting frustrated with each other and began to talk louder and louder, drowning out everyone else.

However, I was able to listen carefully and figure out what he was saying. When I shouted out a translation, he was very excited and nodded his head quickly and everyone laughed. After this incident, my mother thought I was amazing and finally had respect for my Chinese skills.

A FEMALE-DOMINATED
SOCIETY

Lugu Lake is one of the biggest and most famous landmarks in Yunnan, which was originally inhabited and still largely populated by the Mosuo People. It is on a high plateau in the northwest of Yunnan, a remote location hard to access by any means. When we went there, we had to take a crowded bus for almost ten hours—well, it ended up being a bit more than ten hours because the road near Lugu Lake was not completed yet and at more than a few sites we had to wait for construction crews to clear a path before we could cross. During one of the times that we were waiting, we had the option to take a rowboat across the lake to a small island with a house on it. The house had belonged to Dr. Joseph Rock, an American botanist who went to Yunnan in the early twentieth century, and study the many tribes inhabiting the area.

Finally, in the late afternoon, we arrived at the town. It was right on the edge of Lugu Lake—the shore was less than a hundred feet from the road. It was a small town, with only a few small shops, restaurants, and hotels, and we managed to find a hotel before it got too dark. When it did get dark, it was pitch-black except for the star and moon-light, and its reflection on the lake's gentle ripples. Walking around for a few minutes and observing the beauty of the darkened sky, I felt a flash of loneliness as well as happiness. It was a very strange life experience since I grew up mostly in a big city, and nature had seldom been so close to me. It was so quiet and peaceful, time seemed to stand still here—but it won't last long, since a small airport for tourists has been under construction due to so many people who are attracted by its mysterious customs.

The Mosuo house is the home of the whole family, including grandmother, her children and grandchildren, and is arranged in a rectangle of rooms around a large central courtyard. The women in the house do most of the work and make all the decisions. Fortunately for my dad, he was not a Mosuo, so he could make his own decisions.

Most interestingly, they do not have marriage. Men go to women's houses at night and climb through the window of the woman's room, and leave in the morning. Therefore, no marriage needed, no divorce either. After the woman gives birth, the children are raised by the mother and mother's brothers. This female-dominated society is believed to be the only place like it left on earth. The American botanist Dr. Joseph Rock was so fascinated by these unique people, he stayed for most of his life to study as a sociologist.

A man comes to his woman's room through the window at night and leaves in the morning.

TIGER-LEAPING GORGE

Tiger-Leaping Gorge is in Yunnan. It is a deep canyon, through which runs a length of Chang Jiang, also known as Yangtze River, one of China's two most famous and biggest rivers. Tiger-Leaping Gorge is divided into three parts: upper, middle, and lower. The upper section is the easiest to hike, with only a relatively safe hiking path which goes up and down the mountain on the high side of the small vehicle road—nothing special, and nowhere to see the water of the river up close. The middle section is perhaps the most popular destination for hikers. It includes trails on both sides of the road, including one on the other side of the road that goes all the way down to the river. The lower section is the hardest and the only one completely inaccessible by vehicles, but it leads to Tibet. We would have gone all the way down, but we did not have time—we had already bought plane tickets for the following night to Chengdu.

We hired a driver to drive us in and pick us up, and along the way we saw the construction that they were doing. According to residents, the road had been under construction for ten years, and they had decided again to widen and lengthen it due to the crowd of tourists. The construction made our short drive a lot longer and a lot bumpier than reasonable, as well as throwing so much dust that the air was white. Dynamite was a constantly recurring sound, sounding like thunder in the clouds, behind the mountains and valleys. The forest and river were pure, but the construction zone was chokingly dusty and full of the drone of generators and heavy machinery. Already its influence was beginning to be felt on the environment. All of this, the commercialization and standardization of once-unique, beautiful landscapes, and the pollution and destruction of once-pure, undisturbed, quiet environments, just for more tourist money. Thankfully, our driver was skillful enough to maneuver the van past all of the other large trucks and got us there with enough time left over to hike down to the river.

Apparently, the trail that goes to the river in middle Tiger-Leaping Gorge is maintained by an old Naxi woman who lives right next to the start of the trail and hikes along it every day picking up trash, cleaning up debris, and trimming the foliage. Her efforts are not supported by the government, so at the start of the trail she will ask for a $10 RMB/person donation—almost $1.50 USD. As evidenced by the guestbook where we stayed (Tina's Guest House), she is very persistent and will chase you for several minutes if you refuse to pay. Those people, believing it was a scam, ignored her, but when they found out the story later, they felt guilty and returned to pay.

Maintaining that trail is no easy task, either. Although it is not very long, it is still a hard climb, steep and narrow, covered in slippery dirt and gravel. Even me and my parents, who all have had some experience hiking, almost slipped and fell a few times. When we got to the bottom, the rushing of the river was louder than ever. The water moved rapidly, and the stories of people falling in and being drowned or dashed to death against the rocks, their dead bodies seen floating by downriver, seemed perfectly plausible. The legend of Tiger-Leaping Gorge is that there was a tiger being chased by a hunter, and when the tiger reached the river, it jumped onto a rock in the middle and then onto the other side of the river, evading the hunter. Nobody ever seems to be able to agree on which rock it was, but at the bottom of the trail we were on, we came across a large rock in the middle of the river, which could be accessed by an unsafe-looking wooden bridge made of tree branches tied together. A sign said it had been made by another local family, and asked for a $10 RMB donation, but there was nobody around to take our money, so we kept it. Being the adventurous people we are, we decided to cross the surprisingly strong-feeling bridge and lie on top of the rock for a few minutes. It was quite comfortable—not too cold, but with a nice breeze and coolness emanating from the river. At that moment, I felt as if I was at one with nature, and suddenly had a desire to build my own log cabin by the river and live there forever.

On the way back up, we found the "sky stairway" that we had been hearing about. It was a short section of the path that was almost vertical, really just a ladder, with nothing but a steel frame behind the climber to protect them from falls. If anybody was too scared to climb up it, there was a longer, more level path right next to it, but all three of us climbed up the sky stairway. Halfway up, my water bottle fell out of my jacket pocket and almost hit my parents, who were following right below me, luckily, no one was hurt. We were too tired to go back down to look for it; it was already in need of replacement, and it had probably been destroyed, anyway. That night, thoroughly exhausted, we settled into our beds at Tina's and prepared for tomorrow's hike back.

PART VIII

GOD'S COUNTRY

May 2010

MALA SPICY & AN ILLEGAL
TUK-TUK RIDE

We flew from Lijiang to Chengdu, Szechuan, a city famous especially for mapo tofu, a spicy dish of tofu in a red chili sauce with vegetables and beef, which my mom had been making at home with tomatoes and vegetables in place of beef. I was disappointed to learn that the traditional version did not have tomatoes, since they are one of my favorite foods. Of course, for our first meal, we had to try some real mapo tofu. As soon as we were successful in ordering it vegetarian, we were surprised. The flavor was quite different from anything we had ever tried before, particularly due to the use of Szechuan peppercorns, small, peppercorn-shaped fruits which, while unrelated to true peppercorns, lent a mouth-numbing and citrusy, although not too spicy, flavor to the dish. This is the origin of the "numb-spicy" phrase coined to describe many Szechuan dishes. Szechuan peppercorns were a staple in Szechuan cuisine, and this was not the only meal in which we encountered them. At first, I found the numbness and flavor distasteful, but after a few meals, it began to grow on me. It was certainly unique and we were unlikely to taste it anywhere else.

While in Szechuan, we visited Chengdu and ChongQing, as well as Emei Mountain, Leshan's Giant Buddha statue, Dujiang dam, and Dufu's home, which had been made into a large museum and memorial to Dufu. The original home was destroyed long ago, but there are recreations in its place.

Our first stop was Dujiang dam, just outside of Chengdu. As was typical in most of mainland China, transportation was less than easy to figure out, and crowded with more than a reasonable amount of people. After spending too much money on a bus to the area that Dujiang Dam was in, we got off the bus and had no idea what to do. Dujiang Dam was obviously nowhere within walking distance, and we had no idea how to get there. Oh yeah, and it was raining—fortunately, not very hard. After a quick conversation with the local people, we had deduced which bus to take to get to the entrance of Dujiang Dam national park/ museum/memorial/tourist attraction. Unfortunately, that did not make things any easier. Waiting at the bus stop were hundreds of people, most of who were trying to get on the same bus as we were. After more than ten minutes, a bus on the right route finally arrived. The three buses we witnessed, being unable to hold hundreds of people at a time, each filled up quickly before we left in search of a taxi. Unfortunately, taxis proved almost as hard to find. Eventually, we managed to wave down a tuk-tuk, except this was one of the smaller ones, with forward-facing seats and an electric motorcycle engine powering the rear wheels. It was also meant for two people, and we had three fully-grown people. We ended up making the whole journey across the city on barely-sufficient power, barely clinging on to our seats, with my mom almost completely hanging off of one side. At least this time we did not have luggage to carry.

Unfortunately, the street in front of Dujiang Dam was rife with police, and apparently, there are actually laws in China restricting the number of tourists you can have on your frankencycle-turned-taxi. All we knew was that a police officer approached our driver, who had assured us that he could take all three of us at once. They yelled at each other in the barely comprehensible local dialect (almost completely incomprehensible when yelling); and the police officer approached the driver's vehicle and let all of the air out of the tires while the driver watched helplessly. My mom, feeling sorry for the driver and thoroughly convinced that a deflated tire could affect the driver's business greatly, felt responsible and ended up giving the driver a tip much bigger than the original fare. I disagreed with my mother's action and thought it a waste of money, but my mother explained to me later, it was a great opportunity of practicing Di Zi Gui, "treating all the elders like your own parents or grandparents." My mother said, "It's bad enough that the driver has to work at such an old age, with the misfortune of a broken tire, how can we ignore him and move on with our own easy life?" I was touched and felt that I should learn to be more sensitive to the hardships of others, and contemplate more often on Di Zi Gui to enable me to apply sage teaching to my real world.

HEAVEN ON EARTH

Szechuan is known today as Tianfuzhiguo—roughly translated to Heaven on Earth, or God's Country. This is because of its remarkable weather and geographic position, in the middle of a ring of mountains where it is protected from enemy attack, as well as its extreme agricultural fortitude—nearly anything will grow in Szechuan. However, things were not always this way. During the Warring States Period (406–221BC), people who lived along the banks of Szechuan's Min River were plagued by annual flooding. Qin governor Li Bing investigated the problem and discovered that the river was swelled by fast-flowing spring melt-water from the local mountains that burst the banks when it reached the slow-moving and heavily silted stretch below.

One solution would have been just to build a dam, but Li Bing had also been charged with keeping the waterway open for military vessels to supply troops on the frontier, so he also proposed to construct an artificial levee to redirect a portion of the river's flow and then to cut a channel through Mount Yulei to discharge the excess water upon the dry Chengdu Plain beyond.

Li Bing received a large sum of silver for the project from King Zhao of Qin and set to work with a team said to number tens of thousands. The levee was constructed from long sausage-shaped baskets of woven bamboo filled with stones known as Zhulong, held in place by wooden tripods known as Macha. The massive construction took four years to complete and was all done without any modern machinery, using only basic tools, strength, and ingenuity.

Cutting the channel proved to be a far greater problem as the tools available to Li Bing at the time, prior to the invention of gunpowder, were unable to penetrate the hard rock of the mountain. To overcome this obstacle, Li Bing used a combination of fire and water to heat and cool the rocks until they cracked and could be removed, burning the mountain with fire then letting the cold river flow onto it. After a long eight years of hard work, a 20 meter (66 ft) wide channel had been gouged through the mountain. When the system was finished, no more floods occurred. The irrigation made Szechuan the most productive agricultural place in China, earning its reputation as "heaven on Earth." Li Bing was loved so much that he became a deity to the people there. Shrines and exhibits were built in memory of Li Bing.

Li Bing spent his whole life on this project. Its construction is also credited with giving the people of the region a laid-back attitude toward life; by eliminating disaster and insuring a regular and bountiful harvest, it left them with plenty of free time. The dam is so strong that without much maintenance it has already lasted more than 2,000 years. Even in 2008, after an earthquake with a magnitude of 8.0—the epicenter of which was right next to Dujiang Dam—the dam only suffered minor cracks and no major damage.

Walking along the river, listening to the tour guide's explanation, and observing the unique construction that has lasted thousands of years, I was inspired deeply by Li Bing's devotion and spirit, and also admired his remarkable engineering technique and wisdom.

After we took the new high-speed train, which had just opened the day before, we arrived back to Chengdu from Dujiang Dam. We saw a truck washing a relatively clean street with rushing water, while other places in China, like Guangxi and Yunnan which we had just visited, were suffering from a severe drought. This lavish and modern city, Chengdu, led us to believe Szechuan's reputation of Heaven on Earth. The clean, modern, laid-back life style made me want to move here.

TRUE DEDICATION & DILIGENT CULTIVATION

At 3,099 meters (10,167 ft), Emei Mountain is the highest of the Four Sacred Buddhist Mountains of China. Geographically, Mt. Emei sits at the western rim of the Szechuan Basin. The patron Bodhisattva of Emei Mountain is Samantabhadra, known in Chinese as Puxian. Puxian is the Bodhisattva of practice and meditation. He is notable for his Ten Vows, which are commonly cited today as a good guideline for beginner Buddhists who are truly set on reaching Buddhahood. The Ten Vows are:

1. To venerate all Buddhas.
2. To praise all the Buddhas.
3. To make abundant offerings.
4. To repent misdeeds and evil karmas.
5. To rejoice in others' merits and virtues.
6. To request the Buddhas to continue teaching.
7. To request the Buddhas to remain in the world.
8. To follow the teachings of the Buddhas at all times.
9. To accommodate and benefit all living beings.
10. To transfer all merits and virtues to benefit all beings.

Emei Mountain is the site of the first temple ever built in China in the Common Era. Going there and seeing all of the deep Buddhist history was really an amazing experience for me and let me see how important Buddhism was in China.

When we went to Emei Mountain, it was very wet, not uncommon for mountains in China. However, it was not only misty and foggy, but actually raining for most of our visit. This made for hard hiking and sub-par views most of the way, but of course, being on Emei Mountain, they were still amazing.

We were able to see many of the ancient Buddhist temples, which had been there since hundreds or even thousands of years ago, and feel the legacy they left. It was as if the air itself was holy.

However, no amount of holiness could lie undisturbed by monkeys. And along the trails, even in many of the temples, we saw monkeys in droves. We had never seen monkeys so up-close before, besides in a zoo, and naturally, I was intrigued. They were climbing all over the trees lining the trail, and some of them scurried along the handrail. Occasionally, one would even venture across the trail to get to the other side. Having never seen them in such close proximity before, we were fascinated. Just like with everything else unique in China, my mom wanted a picture, and this time, I actually agreed with her.

My dad and I found one of the many monkeys sitting on the railing and sidled over next to it while my mom pointed the camera at us. What we did not expect, however, was for the monkey to reach its hand into my jacket pocket and pull it out, looking for food. I was more than surprised, with nothing in my pocket, the monkey held on tightly for a few seconds, then let go after he was sure there was nothing inside. Luckily, I was not hurt, and this shocking moment had made me realize why there are signs everywhere to warn the tourist not to feed the monkeys.

Robbed by a monkey in Emei Mountain, Szechuan.

After the attempted robbery by a monkey, we continued hiking, and eventually we made it to the top, where there was a giant golden statue of Puxian Bodhisattva. However, the visibility was only a few feet because it was so cloudy. My mom suggested that we chant Puxian Bodhisattva's name and bow to him, and so we did. When we were done, the clouds and fog were thinner, although still far from clear. But we were able to make out the top of the statue neverthe-less, and it was magnificent. Even in the cloudy sky,

Puxian Bodhisattva seemed to shine, and the bright gold on top of the white marble felt like they belonged in heaven—or Western Pure Land—itself.

Puxian Bodhisattva and his vows are a great guideline for every person to follow, and looking at him and hearing his story inspired me. If he could do it, I thought, why couldn't I? After all, every Buddha was once a mundane being just like me. All it takes is true dedication and effort and diligent cultivation to reach Buddhahood.

NEVER GIVE UP

Although Emei Mountain is actually one of the four holy mountains of China, it was not all we wanted to see in the area. Emei Mountain and its encompassing city is actually a county which is part of Leshan Prefecture, and the urban area of Leshan itself is actually home to Leshan's giant Buddha. Leshan lies at the confluence of two rivers, where they merge to become three, which was another spot in Szechuan which experienced frequent flooding. Miraculously, Leshan's giant Buddha, despite its age, was also completely undamaged by the 2008 Szechuan earthquake, which devastated just about everything else in the area.

Construction was started in 713 AD, led by a monk named Haitong. He hoped that the Buddha would calm the turbulent waters that plagued the shipping vessels traveling down the river. When funding for the project was threatened, he is said to have gouged out his own eyes to show his piety and sincerity. During the Buddha's construction, he lived in a small dark cave on the mountain next to the site and practiced an ascetic lifestyle. After his death, however, the construction was stalled due to insufficient funding. About seventy years later, a government official decided to sponsor the project and the construction was completed by Haitong's disciples in 803 AD. After the completion of the giant Buddha, miraculously, flooding in the area went down significantly.

Visiting the giant Buddha, we were able to see the actual cave that Master Haitong lived in when he was trying to build the giant Buddha: it was extremely dark and looked uncomfortable. It was scary, like a tomb in a cave. But Master Haitong lived there every day. His devotion and perseverance are a constant example and reminder for everybody who lives to pursue what is right and work hard at it, never giving up no matter what hardship or opposition lies ahead.

Some may wonder why Haitong gouged out his eyes, arguing that such an act would be unfilial, damaging the body gifted to him by his parents. However, Haitong was not hurting himself for personal desire, but out of sincere pleading to finish a great and noble project. In Chinese history, there are many people who have been so sincere as to lose major body parts in the name of nobility. One legend deals with Hui Ke, the first disciple of the legendary Da Mo, First Patriarch of Zen Buddhism in China, the one responsible for introducing Zen Buddhism to China.

Da Mo was a very diligent and sincere monk himself, and was determined to reach Buddhahood; reasoning that he could help infinitely more beings as a Buddha than as a human, he took no disciples. At that time, Master Hui Ke, who was seeking enlightenment and, hearing of Da Mo's reputation, asked him for help. Da Mo ignored him, but still Hui Ke would not leave, and he knelt in the snow for seven days and nights outside the cave that Da Mo practiced in. Da Mo said that he would not accept Hui Ke as a disciple until the snow turned red. To demonstrate the depth of his dedication and sincerity Hui Ke cut off his arm, with the blood turning the snow red. He was immediately accepted as a disciple and eventually became Da Mo's successor.

The Giant Buddha in Leshan. Construction was led by a monk named Haitong. He is said to have gouged out his own eyes to show his piety and sincerity when the funding was threatened.

THE LONG RIVER

A few days later, we were on a cruise ship, baffled souls heading to a fabled land. Before you get jealous, remember that this was a cruise ship in mainland China and we were trying to save as much money as possible, so we tried to enjoy the trip in spite of the unpleasant environment on the ship. After all, we were going somewhere legendary in China, arguably second only to the Great Wall itself. We were taking a cruise on the Yangtze River, from Chengdu's sister city, Chonqing, all the way to Hubei province's Yichang, a relatively unremarkable city.

The Yangtze River is the longest river in all of Asia, and the third longest in the world. In fact, its Chinese name is not Yangtze, but Chang Jiang, which literally translates to "Long River." Yangtze was the name of a village and ancient ferry crossing along the river, and Western missionaries heard this name and applied it to the entire river.

The Yangtze River has long been a fabled waterway in Chinese culture. Evidence of human activity dating more than 27,000 years ago has been found in the Three Gorges area. Although the Yellow River region was richer and more developed at that time, the milder climate and more peaceful environment made the Yangtze River area more suitable for agriculture.

After the beginning of the Han Dynasty, the Yangtze River started to become more and more important to

China's economy. The establishment of irrigation systems, most notably the Dujiang Dam, made agriculture very stable and productive. By the Song dynasty, the areas along the Yangtze River had become the wealthiest and most developed parts of the country, especially in the lower reaches of the river, closer to China's eastern shore, this region called Jiangnan provided a third to a half of the nation's revenues early in the Qing dynasty.

Until the railroads were built in the twentieth century, the Yangtze River was the primary artery of China's inland transportation system. Without the river, there was really no other way to reach inland China besides walking. The Chinese saw this and capitalized on it with a system of canals and irrigation, dating to ancient times and stretching as far as Beijing.

The Yangtze River was also the site of many legendary stories, and the origin of more than one famous ancient Chinese tradition. Many men famous in China's mythology and history were, at some point in their lives, at the Yangtze River. Perhaps the most famous person to visit the Yangtze River was Li Bai.

In 725 AD, when he was in his mid-twenties, Li Bai sailed down the Yangtze River. His love of the river's beauty was so deep that he had inspired the Chinese people with great imagination and appreciation for the Yangtze River through his poems. According to legend, he was drowned attempting to embrace the moon's reflection. If you are wondering how anybody could be so foolish, remember that Li Bai was also famous for enjoying liquor. Most of his famous poems were believed to have been written after drinking, and in one of the most famous, he even invited the moon and his own shadow to drink with him, which deeply depicted the loneliness of his soul.

Before his untimely death, he wrote many poems mentioning the Yangtze River, the most famous of which talks about hearing the calls of monkeys as he sailed his boat downriver from BaiDi city to Jiangling. The poem has been translated as follows:

> *At daybreak I leave BaiDi amidst clouds aglow,*
> *A thousand miles to Jiangling is a mere day's flow.*
> *Whilst monkeys cry incessantly from bank to bank,*
> *I have skiffed past a myriad mountains row after row.*

Traveling on the same route as those ancient poets, thinking of the famous poems that my mom had made me recite when I was little, I was very excited, expecting monkeys, especially after my close-up experience with monkeys on Emei Mountain. To our disappointment, we heard not a single monkey during our cruise. Perhaps it was due to the Three Gorges Dam's effects, or perhaps due to over-hunting, overdevelopment, or climate change, or maybe all of above. As our boat sailed down, the lack of wildlife, especially monkey calls, that was so famously passed down for over a thousand years in Li Bai's poem, and of course the magnificent towering mountain view of Yangtze River, can never be seen again, the changing face in China deepening our sorrow.

THE ORIGIN OF DRAGON BOAT RACING

Besides Li Bai, the most notable figure associated with the Yangtze River is Qu Yuan, China's first great patriotic poet as well as a great statesman, ideologist, diplomat and reformer.

Qu Yuan lived during the Warring States Period, during which the seven individual kingdoms, Qi, Chu, Yan, Han, Zhao, Wei and Qin, contended with each other for supremacy and rule. Qu Yuan, who lived in the Chu State, was trusted by King Huai and did much to assist the king in governing the state. Following reformation in the Qin state, the Qin gained in strength and invaded the other six states. Qu Yuan suggested an alliance with Qi in order to resist Qin. However, this was rejected by some of the ministers as they could see that they would lose some of their power and privileges. They made false accusations against Qu Yuan that were believed by King Huai. The misguided monarch became alienated from his valued advisor and sent him into exile as a consequence.

In the years that followed, Huai, lacking the wise counsel of Qu Yuan, was deceived by the Qin into thinking that they could live together in peace. However, King Huai was subsequently detained by the Qin State for years until his eventual death. King Huai was succeeded to the throne by his son, who was even more fatuous than his father had been. He disregarded Qu Yuan's advice not to surrender to the Qin. Qu Yuan was exiled to even further away than before.

In 278 BC, upon learning that the Chu State had been defeated by the Qin, Qu Yuan, in great despair and distress, ended his life by drowning in the Miluo River, a tributary of the Yangtze, in the northeastern part of Hunan Province. Qu Yuan was a true patriot. He was so distressed by seeing the corruption of the government and being unable to help that he sacrificed his own life to do the impossible task of trying to awaken the king from his ignorance. In his legacy, we have his story, which is remembered and celebrated by all Chinese, and the poems he wrote, many of which are still famous even today.

According to legend, after Qu Yuan drowned, the villagers desperately wanted to save his body, and raced their dragon boats along the river looking for it. Eventually, when they couldn't find the body, they gave up and wrapped rice up in bamboo leaves and threw it into the river to feed the fish, hoping to save Qu Yuan's body from the indignity of being eaten by fish. Now, every year, to memorialize Qu Yuan's legacy, the Chinese eat Zongzi, rice wrapped in bamboo leaves, and have dragon boat races during the annual Dragon Boat festival, or Duanwu festival.

Qu Yuan's story is only one of the many legends surrounding the Yangtze River, but it is almost unanimously viewed as the most influential and famous.

FLOODED HISTORY

Baidi City, the City of White Emperor or Baidi Temple, is another one of the important historical sites we visited.

In ancient times, revered poets including Libai and Dufu visited and wrote famous poems here, earning Baidi City the colloquial unofficial moniker "Poem City." There are also many historic sites such as Wuhou Ancestral Temple (the Temple of General Guan Yu of the Three Kingdoms Period, 220–280 AD) and Tuogu (Entrusting Sons) Hall, where Liu Bei entrusted his son to Zhuge Liang. Liu Bei was the king of the Shu Kingdom, and he had failed in battle and become fatally ill. Before his death, he entrusted his son to his prime minister, Zhuge Liang, at this very hallowed city.

Baidi City is also the site of many legends and stories that make it famous among the Chinese people.

After the completion of the Three Gorges Dam, Baidi City had been surrounded by the rising water level, becoming an island. Although it was once connected to the shore, we had to cross a long bridge to get there.

The Three Gorges Dam was completed on October 30, 2008. It produces electricity, increases the river's shipping capacity, and reduces the potential for floods downstream by providing flood storage space, but at a terrible cost—worse than any monetary price could ever be.

The Chinese government officially regards the project as a historic engineering, social and economic success, with its advanced design and electrical power production, but the dam flooded archaeological and cultural sites and displaced some 1.3 million people. It is also causing significant ecological changes, including an increased risk of landslides. Because of its undeniable disadvantages, the dam has been a controversial topic both in China and abroad. Is its electrical power, however plentiful, worth the displacement of more than 1 million people and the eternal loss of sites deeply rooted in China's history? Although as many relics as possible were moved and saved, undiscovered artifacts were inevitably lost, and some things, such as the actual locations of artifacts, could not be relocated.

THIRD CLASS BETTER THAN FIRST CLASS?

In this cruise, we had booked three tickets, two in first class for my parents and one in third class for me. If we found third class unbearable, I could just sleep in one of my parents' beds, and we would save money on tickets, we reasoned. The first class tickets were almost twice as expensive, but when we boarded the ship, we were unpleasantly surprised. Perhaps the dilapidated hotel that the travel agency was operating out of should have been a clue to us, but we had booked the tickets through our hotel in Chengdu, without having seen the travel agency in person.

The room my parents stayed in was dirtier than anywhere we had stayed so far. It was even dirtier than the project-building apartment we stayed in in Macao. As a "luxury" measure, there was carpeting in the first-class rooms, but in rural China, they did not even have vacuum cleaners. We saw sunflower seed shells still on the floor from before we got there, and there was even a blood-colored smear on the wall. The bathroom also smelled like a septic tank, perfuming the whole room. With disbelief, my parents called the employees, who were easily able to sweep up the sunflower seeds, but unfortunately, they could not do anything about the smell or stains in the carpet and the wall.

"Oh, god," I thought. "If this is first class, I wonder what third class is gonna be like?" Apprehensively, I made my way downstairs to the ship's lowest level and found my room. When I opened the door, I was in for another surprise. My room had painted wood floors, which were relatively spotless; the bathroom was bigger and didn't smell quite as bad, and, best of all, the five other passengers I had to share it with were all in their early twenties. Needless to say, I enjoyed the trip much more than my parents and ventured up to their room as infrequently as possible. I was reasonably comfortable for the first two days, but three nights without a shower is enough to cause a small amount of discomfort in almost anybody.

The scenery on our cruise was beautiful, but it still came short of the spectacular pictures we had seen because of the drastic change in the water level. In many areas, the river had risen by more than a hundred feet, and the plunging cliffs, deep ravines, and towering mountain peaks seemed much less deep or towering. Eventually, we arrived at Yichang and set off on more long bus rides to Yichang's downtown, intending to find our bus station to Wuhan for that night.

THE FAR HORIZON

At midnight, we arrived in Wuhan. From here, we would be taking an airplane to Shanghai. But our flight was not until that night, so we had a whole day to explore Wuhan. Therefore, we booked a tour guide and rode around the city, going to some of its more famous spots. Most notable of these is the Yellow Crane Tower. The Yellow Crane Tower, which has actually been rebuilt many times, is considered one of the Four Great Towers of China. In its modern version it has the appearance of an ancient tower but is built of modern materials and includes an elevator to each of the four floors.

From the top of the Yellow Crane Tower, almost the whole city of Wuhan is visible. Because it is situated on a hill, it towers above most of the other buildings, and on a clear day, the Yangtze River and the bridges crossing it are also visible. There are many legends about the Yellow Crane Tower, and it was made famous by an eighth-century poem written by the Tang Dynasty poet Cui Hao called "Yellow Crane Tower." The poem can be roughly translated into English as:

> *Long ago a man rode off on a yellow crane, all*
> *that remains here is Yellow Crane Tower.*
> *Once the yellow crane left it never returned,*
> *for one thousand years the clouds wan-*
> *dered without care.*

The clear river reflects each Hanyang tree, fragrant grasses lushly grow on Parrot Island.
At sunset, which direction lies my hometown?
The mist-covered river causes one to feel distressed.

The poem may seem to be a simple story about a man departing from Yellow Crane Tower, but it actually has deeper meaning. The "man" symbolizes ancient saints and sages, philosophers and leaders such as Confucius, Buddha, or Jesus. His departure implies that these philosophers and visionaries have left us and will never return, but their wisdom and teachings are left behind. The question "which direction lies my hometown?" represents the eternal question of humankind, "where do we come from?" or "what is the purpose of life?" In the poem, it is implied that the "man" rode off to return to his own hometown, which is actually not a physical location, but the same as ours—Pure Land, or Nirvana, or Heaven. If a person is asking this question, then it shows that he has hope and will look for the way to return to the "hometown" and unite with the ancient sages.

Even the great poet Li Bai wrote a poem about Yellow Crane Tower titled "Seeing off Meng Haoran for Guangling at Yellow Crane Tower:"

My old friends said goodbye to the west, here at Yellow Crane Tower,
In the March's cloud of willow blossoms, he's going down to Yangzhou.

The lonely sail is a distant shadow, on the
*   edge of a blue emptiness,*
All I see is the Yangtze River flowing to the far
*   horizon.*

As I listened to the tour guide's introduction of those thousand-year-old stories, I thought of my childhood. I did not recognize the poems, but somehow they seemed familiar—like my mother had once made me recite them. Perhaps she did. Either way, I was anxious to go home...

"Attention, Sean Gallgher, please report to the main entrance on the first floor, your family is waiting for you." All of a sudden, my mother's voice cut through the sound of the crowd over a loudspeaker. I woke up from my dream and realized that I had lost my parents in the "mountain sea of people." Rushing down to the first floor, I saw my mom waiting by the front entrance, almost buried by the noise and crowd...

PART IX

RISING FROM ASHES

June 2010

MY MOM SCREWS UP

In the airport, our flight was delayed for many hours, so the airline offered us free dinner. However, when we went to the counter, our food was not ready yet. It was crowded, so when I turned back to go sit down, I did not notice my parents going in the opposite direction. I sat on the floor near the counter, which was not a sitting area although many people were leaning or sitting there and was apparently in some kind of corner behind a lot of people. After sitting down, I looked up, but I did not see my parents behind the crowd of people. "Oh well," I thought, "they'll come back in fifteen minutes to pick up the food, and I'll find them then." Then, I promptly woke up the Asus Eee Netbook we had purchased a few months earlier in Taiwan and continued my fruitless attempts at literature, disregarding my parents' absence. Unfortunately, they did not see me, and for the next thirty minutes, they traversed the whole airport looking for me.

After those thirty minutes, I had written about two disconnected, worthless sentences when my parents suddenly appeared in front of me with an accelerated heartbeat and an angry expression. That was never a good thing, and surely, if I had given the aforementioned situation any thought at all, I could have anticipated this happening. Parents, being parents, are always worried about something happening to their kid. In a big city of a foreign country, being separated is never a good thing, especially when the whole family only has one working cell phone. Deep inside, I knew I should follow my parents all the time and should have found them immediately when I noticed that we had gotten separated, but I didn't feel like running through crowds of people, and I didn't think it would be so critical when they had arranged to come back to pick up food in fifteen minutes. I didn't think about the fact that I was not easily visible and, as I learned later, they had in fact come back to the counter to look for me, and because of my inconspicuous position, they didn't see me and moved on to search elsewhere.

The worry and fear that grips a parent when they cannot find their child is a truly horrible thing, and I have learned that, even if it seems like it does not matter, one should never leave without informing the people they are traveling with. My parents delivered a big lecture about when you are with other people, always make sure to communicate thoroughly and surely, so that you confirm that they have received your message.

So, our flight from Wuhan to Shanghai was delayed for a few hours. During the delay, an airport staff member came to ask my mother to help them explain to an English-speaking passenger, who obviously was very confused with the delay. And there was an Indian passenger who also came to my mother asking for help. My mother encouraged me to volunteer, so I went to help him translate. This involved going back out through airport security and getting a "proof of delay" or something from the airline counter for his connecting flight, but unfortunately, I forgot that my passport was still in the waiting area with my parents. Therefore, they would not let me back in, and the Indian passenger had to go in and get my passport for me. At that time, my mom was thinking she would wait for my dad's return from the restroom and then go with him. But under the pressure of the Indian guy's anxiety, my mom hesitated a little bit then handed him my passport. A few minutes later, she realized that she had just given my passport to a stranger. She started getting worried and ran after him...

Luckily, nothing bad happened. But it became a focal topic of the trip. We laughed at my mother's mistake, but she just acknowledged her mistake without anger. My father pointed out how her attitude was different from mine because she was not defensive and aggressive, and admitted her mistake, while I get offended very easily and never admit my mistakes. My mother's silliness became a lesson invaluable to my thinking and attitude of life.

Searching THE FAR *Horizon*

EXPO 2010 & A RENDEZVOUS

In Shanghai, we again encountered my cousin Megan, whom we had first seen in Anhui. Megan had learned Mandarin in college and had recently decided to go to mainland China to teach English. This was quite the coincidence, considering that we never planned either of these rendezvous. We had just decided to go to Anhui when we found out that Megan had just gotten a job there, and when we were going to Shanghai, we called her to tell her our plans when she revealed that she had just secured a job there and would be arriving about a week before our visit. Out of all the provinces and cities in China, she just happened to be at the two exact same ones that we would pass through, at the exact time we were passing through them. I guess this is just proof of the karma and connection between certain people. Some people you can search for forever, and never find them, and some, you can pay no effort at all and still run into them wherever you go.

With Megan, we went to the world-famous EXPO 2010, or World's Fair. It was the first time in history that China had been chosen to host the World's Fair, and, just like during the 2008 Olympics, it was determined to show the world what it was capable of. A whole swath of land was set aside specifically for the fair, and billions of dollars were spent on the construction and coordination of the event, making this

172

the most expensive World's Fair in history. However, although it was obviously an extremely capable feat that the Chinese government had pulled off, the Expo left many visitors, especially those from the western hemisphere or who had been to previous world's fairs, unimpressed.

It was not that Expo 2010 was too small, or too poorly constructed, or not spectacular enough, but more the overall coordination and discomfort of it.

China, a nation of billions, is one of the most populous countries in the world, and much of this population lives in poverty. So when the Expo came to Shanghai, billions of people saw it as their primary opportunity to see the outside world and foreign people for much cheaper than a plane ticket, and flocked to Shanghai. This would have been fine, had they all learned basic manners. Unfortunately, many of them had never left their hometowns in their lives, and in most of rural China, pushing fighting in lines, talking extremely loudly are very common, so the Expo was full of behaviors like this. While I, having already seen half of China, including some very rural towns that even native Chinese have never heard of, did not mind too much, and was certainly not surprised, most Westerners were completely appalled.

Add to this hour-long lines, usually lasting between one hour for countries no one cares about like Kazakhstan, to over eight hours (sometimes, even twelve hours) for countries that were either extremely popular, like Japan, or that had spent a lot of money, like Saudi Arabia, and it would be safe to say that Expo was an unpleasant experience for the uninitiated.

Although I also didn't mind too much waiting in lines under the hot sun for nine hours (what we did to get into Saudi Arabia's twelve-minute presentation of a pavilion), I agreed that it was ridiculous how, due to the impossibly long lines, one one-day ticket could only get a visitor into perhaps two or three pavilions if they decided to visit a popular one, if lucky.

As for coordination, the World's Fair was traditionally an example of a great event where countries would come together in unity to learn from and about each other's ways and traditions, and there would be novelties and new inventions debuting. Expo 2010, however, just seemed like a competition for who could build the best pavilion, and many of the pavilions failed to provide even basic information about their countries' cultures and traditions.

Personally, I found the Expo to be enjoyable overall, learning a few things about other countries' cultures and getting to see real artifacts and items from various countries, as well as meeting their people. Having never been to a World's Fair before, I did not have any particular expectations, and although I may go to other, better world fairs in the future, I will never forget my first one in Shanghai 2010.

FIRST TO SACRIFICE & LAST
TO RELAX

After the Expo, we met my cousin Ray and went together to Suzhou, a historic town only a few hours away from Shanghai. Suzhou is famous for its numerous gardens and courtyards, which are said to be among the most beautiful in the world. There is one courtyard which is famous for being beautiful, but the original builder is not famous at all. The original builder was a government official who, upon retirement, built the garden for his own private use but did almost nothing with his money to help the general public. Therefore, he was not especially celebrated or remembered, and his son lost the whole, extremely large garden gambling. Fan Zhongyan, on the other hand, did not build a personal garden, but is widely remembered and respected today—almost every Chinese person knows his name and story.

Fan Zhongyan was a prominent Song Dynasty government official who was born into poverty in a suburb of Suzhou. Having experienced extreme poverty himself, Fan Zhongyan made a vow that he would sacrifice himself to suffer before letting others suffer, and would not indulge in unnecessary pleasures until everybody else in the world was happy. He came from a poor family, and his father died when he was young. In the interest of survival, his mother married into another family. Fan Zhongyan, demonstrating his filial piety, told his mother to "wait ten years" for him to pass the Imperial Exam, and he went to a temple and studied. During that time, he ate one bowl of porridge, split into three portions, per day. In less than ten years, he had built such knowledge and wisdom that he was able to pass the Imperial Exam with flying colors. Even when he had become the highest government official, a prime minister, and had enough money to build a magnificent garden of his own, he still lived as frugal as possible, never using even one cent to improve his personal living condition. Instead of indulging in material objects, he used his extra money to support an entire village of more than three hundred families.

Fan also began educational reforms in the 1040s. In ancient China, schools were almost exclusively privately funded and run, and only the elite and wealthy could afford to get an education. Fan Zhongyan, however, believed that education was important for everybody and allocated government funds to education, essentially creating the world's first public education system. In addition to being a great government leader and revolutionary thinker, Fan Zhongyan was also a writer and scholar himself and left many influential works, mostly about philosophy and government.

Even today, almost a thousand years later, all of Fan Zhongyan's descendants are all very fortunate and well respected. According to some researchers, all his descendants have proudly honored learning his spirit of "suffer before other people suffer, enjoy yourself after the whole world has been happy." Fan Zhongyan is considered the most influential scholar next to

Confucius in Chinese history. This is further evidence of the good deeds and karma he accumulated.

In Chinese culture, it is believed that the merit accumulated by ones' ancestors can shelter their descendants. For example, Confucius himself was the product of meritorious families. In Confucius' time, all marriages were prearranged, and the criteria his mother's parents used to choose for their son-in-law was the family's merit. They found a family whose ancestors were all great men who had done many meritorious deeds, and the product of this marriage was Confucius himself, proving that the ancestors' merit affects their descendants.

Another evidence of the Chinese emphasis on merit and filial piety is that, in the ancient times, before the Imperial Exams, the Emperor himself would choose his advisors and officers based on their demonstrating filial piety and merit in their lives, because knowledge without merit is only deleterious.

Fan's selfless, compassionate, and generous attitude made me think of Di Zang Bodhisattva's vow. They all think of only other people's benefit and never put themselves first. I had the honor to know these great stories and visit their memorial sites; I hope I can follow their steps in the coming years. And I believe it serves as an example and goal for everybody, and he will forever be remembered in China as a legend.

THE AWAKENING BELL

Hanshan Temple is famous because of the poem "A Night Mooring by Maple Bridge" by Tang Dynasty poet Zhang Ji. The poem describes a weary traveler passing through Fengqiao, hearing the bells of Hanshan Temple.

The poem is roughly translated as:

> *While I watch the moon go down, a crow caws*
> *through the frost,*
> *Under the shadows of maple-trees a fisherman*
> *moves with his torch;*
> *And I hear, from beyond Suzhou, from the*
> *temple on Cold Mountain,*
> *Ringing for me, here in my boat, the midnight*
> *bell.*

According to the tour guide, Hanshan Temple became so famous only because of this poem from the Tang Dynasty, again one of the poems vaguely in my memory that I might have been forced by my mother to recite. The sound of the bell in Hanshan Temple has rung for thousands of years in Chinese people's hearts. Now that we were here, we "must" ring the bell!

When we got to the bell tower, there was a long line. People were standing around waiting to ring it, and almost everybody who rang it smashed it as hard as they could. The sound was deafening, almost jarring. However, not every sound was so cacophonous. Some people rang it differently, with a firm sureness instead of a violent roughness. When they rang it, they seemed calmer, and the sound was completely different. It reverberated powerfully, like the ripples in a lake, getting gradually quieter with each second. Its sound seemed to linger in the air for minutes and penetrate straight past the eardrums to the heart.

In Buddhism, the bell is symbolic of the truth of Buddha Nature, how, no matter how corrupted and lost a being is, their Buddha Nature will still be alive deep inside of them, waiting to be expanded on. Therefore, there is an idiom to describe the sounds of the morning bell and night drum from a temple as symbols of awakening; the sounds call all the sentient beings still within the illusion of life to arise.

BRUSH WITH DEATH

After exploring Suzhou, my mom found out that Master Yin Guang's temple was in a nearby town. Master Yin Guang was one of the most important Buddhist monks of the early twentieth century, and is still highly respected. He was also the Thirteenth Patriarch of Pure Land Buddhism, and there are many stories about him. We went to the temple to which he once retreated and saw the actual room he lived in.

The room was small and austere, but clean. There was a single-person bed, bookshelf, wooden writing desk, and a word, "death," that he had written, hanging prominently above numerous brush-pen pieces, jumping out to you. The floors were stone, the walls were plain, and simple shades obscured the windows. Master Yin Guang not only lived there, he retreated there for years, never leaving, only having meals delivered by disciples. I found it unimaginable. The room was perhaps only twice as big as my bedroom back home; I could not imagine staying inside for a whole day, let alone years at a time.

Master Yin Guang constantly reminded people that death could come at any moment, and to live every second of life in preparation for death, never doing evil deeds or accumulating bad karma. If a practitioner thought about the possibility of death at any moment, he would be more likely to practice diligently and achieve more.

Along with the word "death" on the wall was another small couplet by the master that stood out:

"Visualize the suffering of hell; determination of cultivation will arise from your heart." Rooted from the Cause and Effect teaching by Buddhas, this sentence hanging on the wall deeply strikes a practitioner. As I believe in Cause and Effect more since the understanding has grown on me during this one year, I have vowed to myself that I should practice more diligently for a better destiny before and after death. After all, diligently practicing sage teachings can benefit both others and me regardless of believing in hell or not.

At Master Yin Guang's temple, we had the good fortune to do volunteer work there, helping to move bricks for the construction of his memorial tower. It was a once-in-a-lifetime experience, and made me feel closer to Master Yin Guang and extremely lucky. As a disembodied voice pointed out, I had no idea how lucky I really was. It was not every day that a memorial tower for a Buddhist Patriarch is built, and they had just started work days before I arrived.

As we worked, I inevitably attracted attention. As the only young person who was not a monk and the only person who did not appear Chinese, I was, to say the least, a curiosity. One man in particular took a keen interest in me and kept asking me questions. Later I found out that he was (unsurprisingly) a diligent and sincere Buddhist practitioner who volunteered at a temple, and he wanted me to help him translate some Buddhist phrases he had come up with into English so he could talk to the tourists. I effortlessly translated everything he gave me, and surprisingly, my mother, who found me at the end of the work session, was astonished by my newfound Chinese skill.

BOWING TO THE PEAK

Before finishing this one-year journey, my mom had another wish to fulfill: to visit Putuo Mountain, another of the four sacred mountains in China. Putuo Mountain's patron saint is Avalokitesvara Bodhisattva, the Bodhisattva of Compassion and Mercy. Avalokitesvara's compassion is a representation of the compassion of all Buddhas and beings. Avalokitesvara is the Bodhisattva who made a great vow to assist sentient beings in times of difficulty, and to postpone his own Buddhahood until he assisted every being on Earth in achieving nirvana. Avalokitesvara is one of the most popular, well-known and respected bodhisattvas in Buddhism.

Putuo Mountain is a small island off the coast of China, a few hours' ride away from Shanghai by bus, then a short boat ride from the shore. At Putuo Mountain, my mother was determined to make a pilgrimage to the top of the highest peak, bowing once for every three steps we took. Fortunately for me, the highest mountain was not that high, but making such a pilgrimage was still a daunting task, and one that I had not the least bit of enthusiasm for.

On our second day there, before 5:00 a.m., we woke up. We had bought kneepads from a mini-mart the day before, and we quietly applied them and started our trek towards the hiking path. Since it was 5:00 a.m., none of the tourist shuttles were running yet, and we had to walk for an hour to the bottom of the tallest trail. Sometime after six, we started, three steps, one bow, up the long staircase to the top of the mountain. In the hour it had taken us to walk there, the rest of the island had woken up and started filtering onto the trails. People turned to look at us, many surprised by my age and ambiguous ethnicity. We even saw a few other groups of people doing the same thing, although the methods varied—some only did a half bow, while some of them did one bow every ten steps.

At Putuo Mountain we made a pilgrimage to the top of the highest peak, bowing once for every three steps we took.

In fact, my mom herself was inspired by some young college students we saw at Jizu Mountain. Talking to them, we had found out that they had started hiking up at 6:00 a.m., bowing once every three steps, and when we saw them at dusk, around 7:00 p.m., they were almost at the top of Jizu Mountain, which is a lot taller than Putuo Mountain. My mom knew many stories about famous monks or historical figures who made pilgrimages, bowing every few steps, but until now, she had never witnessed it in real life, and she was deeply touched by the two young students' devotion and sincerity and vowed to follow it.

At any rate, we finally made it to the top around noon, tired but accomplished. For the rest of the day, we just walked around the pathways more and kept exploring the rest of the island until we left. Unfortunately, we did not have the fortune to see Buddha or even Avalokitesvara Bodhisattva, the patron of Putuo Mountain, whom many visitors claim to have seen. I guess this is just a sign that our practice is not at that level yet and we should keep trying.

FINALLY HOME

Life was great. I felt like I was glowing, almost always happy and in a good mood, and able to do work with much more efficiency and determination. I appreciated my house in Los Angeles now. Sure, it was inconvenient, but it was clean, it had a real toilet and a real washing machine and dryer, and I slept on a real bed in my own room.

After this year-long journey, I have learned that I should not give up easily as I used to and I have to keep living to help the people who need it. Whenever I feel like giving up, I will think of the people I have met, my own friends who live in poverty and solitude, some of whom have already made it to a better life.

I think of Mr. Yan, homeless and broke, with nothing left to lose, but instead of giving up or resorting to crime, he gave all the strength and ability he had left to help others selflessly, and he slowly became the successful man he is today.

I think of those kids in Lujiang, many of whom came from small farming villages, the type of place where few families have enough money to survive, and few children are lucky enough to make it past elementary school. They committed their life to learning about Chinese cultural teachings and following a just, moral path in life, and even if they undergo misunderstandings, they have no choice but to either swallow them and remain in Jushiling or go back to a life of farming, disappointing and shaming their parents by being kicked out.

I think of all the young teenagers I met in big cities like Shanghai and Suzhou, who were still high-school age and immigrated from smaller cities to find opportunity and work to support their families, dreaming of perhaps one day saving enough money to finish school or even college, buying their own houses and cars, going to see other countries and places. Sadly, for many of them, these things will remain a dream. They come to the city from all over, knowing nobody, lonely and overworked, making maybe only a few hundred RMB a month, much of which they send back to their families.

I think of the Foxconn workers, twelve of whom committed suicide in the Shenzhen plant in May of 2010, who work on an assembly line more than ten hours a day with few holidays, chasing the same dream, and then reminded myself that those conditions are considered *good* in China.

I think of the laborers who carry up to a hundred kilograms of rocks, sandbags, or other materials such as food up long mountain roads; and also the other workers who build roads, buildings, or other structures along the mountains we hiked, by hand, with barely more than chisels and hammers.

Compared to them, any difficulties I encounter can hardly be called challenges. And if I really ever fall into a worse condition, then I still won't give up. After all, if I survive the worst of the worst, I will be able to survive anything.

In the past, when I encountered hard times, I thought about these things too, but I could not comprehend them. Now that I have seen the kinds of conditions these people live in, and even made personal friends with many of them, it's more than just hypothetical thoughts, words, and stories in my head. It becomes real and alive.

LIFE & TEA

Sitting in a comfortable high-back chair that my parents recently bought for me, I am thinking back. A story arose from my heart at this moment: During my trip, I happened to pass through a temple in Shenzhen called Hongfa Temple. Hongfa Temple is the biggest temple in Shenzhen, and Master Hsu Yun had been there and been friends with the abbot. Besides these few interesting facts, the temple was nothing special. But, on one of the walls was a story that I will remember forever.

One day, a young practitioner was dissatisfied with his life, which he felt was full of many hardships, and went to a temple, seeking answers from a Buddhist monk. After listening to his stories, the monk calmly said to one of his disciples, "Dharma brother, please bring us some tea and some room-temperature water." When he got the tea, he poured the room-temperature water into cups with tea leaves, stirred it, and told the practitioner to drink. After taking a few sips, he asked the practitioner, "How was the tea?"

"Horrible," the practitioner said. "There was no taste at all—it was just like drinking water!"

The monk simply smiled and motioned again for his disciple to bring a pot of boiling water. He then used the boiling water to make two more cups of tea, and once again instructed the practitioner to drink.

"Now," asked the monk, "How is this tea? Do you taste any difference from the first cup you drank?"

"Yes, of course!" exclaimed the practitioner. "This tea is so fragrant and flavorful! It is much better than the first cup!"

"Aha," explained the monk. "See, this cup of tea is just like life."

"Like... life?" asked the practitioner. "How?"

"You see," said the monk, "the lukewarm water could not make very good tea. The lukewarm water merely moistened the tea leaves, but could not bring out their flavor or fragrance. The tea leaves merely clumped together in the bottom and stayed wrinkled together. The boiling water, however, was able to bring the flavor and fragrance out of the leaves. Its hot temperature caused the leaves to spread out and open up to release their flavor, and the convection of the hot water swirling around in the cup moved the tea leaves around, causing them to be more flavorful. The hot water is just like the hardship of life, and the lukewarm water represents the comfort of life, a life without the tests of hardships, which may not be rewarding. These hardships should be taken as positive experiences and learned from, for it will bring out the best within your inner potential. When life gives you something, do your best to make the best of it," the monk finished, smiling.

My life before this trip was incomplete. Perhaps it was not terrible, but it could have been much better. I never wanted to go on this trip, but when I realized that I had to, whether I wanted to or not, I began to accept it and try to learn from it, and as a consequence, it has become one of the most influential and important events in my life so far. Just like the hot water, this trip was a turbulent "awakening" experience. It scalded me and affected me so greatly that, like a tea leaf, I began to open up and release more of my feelings and emotions. Hopefully, with the experiences I gained in this trip, my life will be as flavorful and meaningful as a hot cup of tea.

Throughout this one-year journey, I was able to go from an angry young man, nervous, apprehensive, and ignorant, to a much calmer, content, aware person. Not only have I prepared myself for any challenge or test of life, but I have also gained much more appreciation for my parents and the sacrifices they made to help me succeed. Probably no other parents would be willing to spend such time, money, and tremendous effort to help their son change his attitude and improve his awareness. I gained not only a much deeper understanding of the Confucius way of life but a true feeling of gratitude for everything my parents did for me, from giving birth to feeding and teaching me for sixteen years to taking me on this trip.

AFTERWORD

It has been almost a year since we have come back from this long trip to China, and we are happy with my son's progress. Just as my son said in the last chapter of this book, this journey has become "one of the most influential and important events" in his life. It was a turbulent "awakening" experience, scalding him and affecting him so greatly that, like a "tea leaf", he began to open up and release his feelings and emotions. I was very surprised to see this writing in his conclusion, and I can see him trying so hard to express himself and look people in the eyes... Although his speech and behavior still displays differences from what is typical, compared to before, he has improved so much in general.

Looking back on the year in China, the difficult times we have encountered because of his Asperger's traits left us many challenges. For instance, some people complained to me of his "roughness" such as his bike riding with sudden, jerky movements, letting doors bang shut after himself, or dropping stuff on a table instead of putting things down gently. His classmates had to re-mop the floor or re-wash the dishes that he had just done, and even though this clumsiness was all related to his body coordination, it was interpreted as rude, impatient, or undisciplined. Based on my experience, I learned to just bite my tongue and apologize when people questioned me because no one would believe my son had any physical problem, since he looked absolutely healthy.

Sometimes, my son did some inappropriate action, like continuing to touch another child's head as a friendly gesture when they are playing, even after the child had pushed him away and he still wasn't aware that he had caused other people's annoyance, it is because he is not used to using verbal communication to express that he likes them. Sometimes he talks to people too closely and incessantly, causing them discomfort when conversing about something he is passionate about. These hidden disabilities with social skills left an extreme challenge for me as well. I tried hard to explain this to him, but he felt I was disgracing him and accused me of being the one who was "different" from the general population. It would be much more effective if others just told him their feelings directly, but it is not easy to find the kind of person who is willing to help at all, and even if I found someone who is willing to help, it would be equally difficult to get them to understand his "hidden disabilities" as to teach my son neuro-typical standards. Most people seem to have a fixed mind, thinking that this was the parent's job, so they would just walk away or avoid interacting with him again and keep the "bad parenting" image in their mind.

Of course, some misunderstandings can turn into a positive teaching moment if someone has the patience to explain to him the "neuro-typical" standards. For example, he does not pay attention to people's response when conveying a message to them, due to lack of "eye contact". Numerous times, I thought I had lost him during this year because he would just disappear and insist that he had told me where he was going after I had found him, until one day at Dancing Cranes Temple, he went to a sports event with Uncle Xu, a volunteer in the temple. He disappeared for more than an hour and insisted that he did tell Uncle Xu where he was going. After almost an hour-long lecture from one of the Venerables, he finally understood better the concept of making sure the message was received by looking in the eyes and observing the response.

His improvements included now seldom answering "I don't know" to people's questions like he used to say all the time; instead, he has become more brave to ask questions and solve problems, a sign of his emotions being released. He no longer sleeps with the alarm ringing for an hour, still lying on the bed in the morning, a sign of his physical recovery. He no longer needs to be supervised for his morning praying, and no longer needs to be reminded of his schedule all the time. Most amazingly, he can complete his assignments and chores independently without the need for us to redo them, such as vacuuming the house, washing dishes, cleaning up his room, etc. We can now garden together on the weekends, cooperating nicely like a "family team". The constant screaming and frustration with each other that I was always so worried might cause the neighbors to call the police almost never happens anymore. We literally gained back the peace in our lives, and I could not be happier for that.

Although my son's progress seems slow and minor, and far from the standards of neuro-typical people, for an Aspergerian or autistic child, this progress is something every parent would die for, especially the part of expressing their feelings and asking for help. That means less misunderstandings and frustration occurring and having more control of life. In other words, there is more possibility for success and an independent life.

One thing I have to emphasize here is that it looks like he seems to have learned so much from this trip based on what he has written in this book. However, how much he really "internalized" is still an unknown question to us. Because one trait of Asperger's is that they may appear to have learned details well but have difficulties to relate what they learned to themselves personally and apply to their real life. However, we are still happy that he can at least organize his thoughts by writing them down. We have learned not to expect too much but believe that things will continue to improve over time.

You may wonder how this one-year trip would affect him. Please allow me to explain the effects in three aspects: Food, Oxygen, and the Mind.

FOOD

A few years ago, I was very impressed by a commercial slogan that said, "You are what you eat", which showed an image of a pear-shaped human with a donut stuck to her butt. When I observed the main diet of meat and dairy products with hormones that most of the population consumes in this country, I realized why pear-shaped figures are so common in our society, and why the average puberty age has been pushed a few years earlier than what it was only decades ago. My son, influenced by this "trend", loved dairy products, chips, and sugary drinks. If this only affected his physical shape, I probably would not have cared so much, but it obviously affected his sinuses badly and made him restless, or mentally "hyper". I did not know it actually affected his brain function as well until we met Brother Mountain, the reflexologist.

How would food affect brain function? According to Dr. Julie A. Buckley, the author of *Healing Our Autistic Children* and a pediatrician whose daughter was also impacted by autism, "the poisons are readily available at your friendly neighborhood grocery store. They are as present as the water we drink. They are as common as the air we breathe. These pervasive toxins in our modern world weaken our immune system and overwhelm our liver, an organ that is charged with expelling toxins from the human body."

As a result, our body stimulates its own defenses and finds other ways, such as skin rashes, to help with expelling the toxins. In my experience, the allergic reaction of hives that I used to suffer with for many, many years was evidence of my overwhelmed liver. The symptoms were gone after I began to eat non-pesticide and non-processed food as much as possible, and stopped taking all chemical pills, including supplements and drugs prescribed by doctors.

My son, when he was one-and-a half years old, also experienced a similar near-fatal acute antibiotic allergy. The reaction was so strong that he had half of his face swollen, which looked so scary that I cried all the way to the doctor's office. The doctor had to give him at least three shots to bring the swelling down and drew blood to see if there was anything wrong in his body. Of course, they neither found anything wrong in his blood, nor admitted to the antibiotic's "poison". My son was back to normal in three days after I stopped giving him the medicine from the doctor and simply gave him vegetable and fruit juice instead. Since then, vegetable and fruit juice has become our family remedy to deal with almost any "sickness" related to the body system's infection or pollution. However, the image of my son's swollen face is still constantly with me, and I always ask myself, if the "outside of his head"- *his face*, had gotten swollen so badly, what happened to the "inside of his head"-*his brain*? Could it have been swollen and damaged too? If the answer is yes, then would that inflamed brain block the path of receiving and sending messages, affecting its function?

Another case of swollen skin caused from food is my husband who developed many itchy bumps on his scalp during the year we were in China. The bumps disappeared after about half a year once we came back, because he is eating healthy home cooking again. He now accepts the concept that his chronic nasal inflammation may also be caused by food toxins like preservatives, pesticides, and additives, and more willingly avoids processed food, as well as most restaurant food. He also tried the excruciatingly painful reflexology after seeing my son's progress.

I can't address enough how bad it is that the food available in our market nowadays has threatened our health so tremendously that even the "organic" processed products contain some preservatives as allowed by the FDA. A few years ago, I had such a bad allergic reaction from "organic soy milk" that my skin was irritated and my eyes were puffy, swollen, red, and itchy— only a few hours after drinking it. It got much worse when I applied the milk to my face assuming it would offer natural soothing to my skin. I almost rushed myself to an emergency room, but didn't, due to my experiences in the past. I knew that they would just give me a drug or shot that appeared to work, but had the side effect of leaving some "poison" in my system as well. I walked around my house looking for a natural solution, maybe an herb, and then I saw aloe vera. I pinched one leaf, extracted its slimy juice and applied it to my face. Almost instantly, I felt its soothing effect and less than half an hour later, my red, puffy, and itchy eyes were back to normal and my face was no longer irritated. I was amazed by Mother Nature, who had cured my "allergy". What a simple solution!

The moment that I started to have an allergic reaction, I thought my health had gotten so bad that my body was even allergic to soy, which has been my favorite food since childhood. To test this, I went to a local store, where only Chinese-style breakfast was sold. I bought one bottle of soymilk, went home and did the same thing: drank it and applied it to my face. This time, nothing happened except the natural sweetness in my throat and the gentle comfort on my skin. By this point, I was pretty sure the organic soymilk had contained some additives. I checked the label and it had twenty-one days until its expiration date, which is impossible for soymilk; any experienced chef can tell you that soymilk will only keep for a few days, even in the refrigerator. I put that bottle in my refrigerator, and after two weeks, it was still fine, so I brought that bottle to the store where I had gotten it. The boss of that store insisted that they used only organic soy to make it and did not add preservatives, but accepted my suggestion to do some investigation. A few days later, I got the answer that confirmed my suspicion: the organic soymilk had an added "food stabilizer", which has no different effect from preservatives, but was given FDA approval.

Most people probably think organic food must be safe, just as I had before. Well, think again. The business style nowadays has expanded in size to meet its demanding market, and the sales area has also extended as far as transportation can reach. Most food we consume today comes from every corner of the earth. How can they keep the food fresh after traveling hundreds, or even thousands of miles without adding something extra?

Some organizations or "Autism Societies" believe that autism is not a mental disease, but a physical illness where the patient's body is at war with itself. Statistics show a very high percentage of autistic patients also suffer from chronic gastrointestinal, immune system, or sinus problems. With the long-term fight against my own allergy and the lasting combat of my son's physical and mental condition; I could not agree more with this theory.

Unlike children who are much weaker and vulnerable and are likely to be impacted by those "pollutions" more immediately, most adults are much more tolerant, until these "poisons" slowly accumulate in their body systems, finding a weak spot to strike, and causing dysfunction or illness. Although the average life expectancy has been extended, people living in the modern life have suffered much more disease than the old time, ADD, autism, cancer, AIDS, Alzheimer's...the list goes on...Have you ever thought of the real cause? I feel like that businesses along with the government have created for the public a scheme of mass genocide without bloodshed. If this is not infuriating to you, well, maybe you do not mind having Alzheimer's, a brain dysfunction disease, or other modern diseases, such as cancer, later on in your life. Maybe you also do not mind that one day the only successful business will be healthcare, especially children's hospitals. What hope will we have for our future if our society has more and more sick children? Isn't this alarming enough for you?

During the year, we stayed mostly in remote areas of China. We followed the simple lifestyle of the local people. They eat simple local food, in season, and almost the same food every day, but stay mostly healthy in general. I once asked a local, how they maintained nutrition and kept their physical energy and health. "What nutrition?" he responded, surprisingly. He said nutrition had never crossed his mind because he believes every piece of land on Earth offers the nutrition its inhabitants need.

When I asked, "What do you do when you get sick? How far is this place to a hospital?" more surprise showed on his face, and he said, "Most people here have never been to a hospital in their whole life. We deal with most of our illnesses with only traditional herbal remedies that were passed down from generation to generation."

I was very impressed by what I heard and observed there. It was a completely different attitude than the people in modern society had, who mostly focus on how to get enough nutrition for their body, yet manifest more health problems than most people in less-developed societies. I think the key to our health nowadays is not what to eat anymore, but *"what not to eat"*.

Finally, I couldn't help to share with you some good news. My son has much better control of his diet after understanding the impact that food has. He no longer sneakily buys junk food at school and is much more content with home cooking. As a result, his sinus problem is almost gone even after stopping reflexology for two months. My son has eventually been persuaded one hundred percent that the food he eats absolutely affects his health immensely. We speculate that the inflamed sinuses were caused by those polluted foods, just like my allergic hives were the product of them. The only difference is my "bumps" occurred on the outside of the body, and my son's "bumps" occurred on the inside. In addition to the nasal polyps, is it possible that the brain, where we can not see, can also grow some kind of "bumps" still undetectable by modern scientific equipment and lead to some dysfunction such as ADHD, Autism and Alzheimer's?

In spite of the progress my son has made at school after this one year trip, he still feels stressed and frustrated due to the high demands of the modern life. We comforted him, "Give yourself ten years to adjust your health! After all, the deep snow was not caused by one day's low temperature, how can we expect one day's sun heat to melt it all?"

OXYGEN

I assume everyone has caught a cold or flu sometime in his or her life. Do you remember when you have had a stuffy nose and headache that makes you feel drowsy, emotionally irritated, or even unable to think, and you just wish for a good long rest? Well, imagine if you had a sinus problem 24/7 for your whole life. How would that make you feel?

When Brother Mountain, the reflexologist, told me that my son's sinus problems prevented his brain from getting enough oxygen to function normally, it started to make sense to me why he felt drowsy all the time, even falling asleep and snoring during a class. He would disregard many of the lectures we delivered to explain how his behavior was very disrespectful, would affect his impression on people, and lead to bad relationships. It started to make sense to me why he had less of, or a slower, response, many times even lacking a response and being called "retarded" or "weird" by his peers. When he drove adults crazy, he was actually fighting with his body and could not think, eventually shutting down his brain and retreating. It also all makes sense now why he got so irritated for seemingly no reason at all when we tried to get his attention. If only he could get enough oxygen, his Asperger's symptoms would reduce accordingly, Brother Mountain promised me. He also promised that he could use his massage to cure 70-80 percent of my son's sinus problem, and that if he had not had tonsil and adenoid surgery, he could have been cured 100 percent.

We all take oxygen for granted, the most essential ingredient for life. But for some people, they have to strive for it and still do not get enough for their body. "When we don't get enough oxygen, our body will shut down its systems and cease its functions. Its breathing gets shorter, pulse rates increase, blood pressure drops, mental capacity is compromised, and we may start to hallucinate. All these symptoms are possible signs of our system and organs shutting down for want of air," Doctor Buckley further states.

Some doctors use hyperbaric therapy, a pressurized oxygen chamber which helps more oxygen dissolve in the patient's blood than at normal atmospheric pressure in order to treat their autistic patients, and have found its effects to be phenomenal. It was reported to "help patients' brains reach sharpened mental acuity or improved cerebral metabolism, making their patients improve by strides in several key, observable areas, including speech, communication, cognitive and sensory awareness, concentration, and sleep patterns."

My son felt a huge difference; though he was not given hyperbaric chamber therapy, he received a very ancient method that is assumed to have been passed down from ancient Egypt: Reflexology. He was observed by many of my friends and family to be less sleepy, show more awareness of his surroundings, have more interaction with people he encounters with a more cooperative attitude and more expression of his feelings. Most importantly, he is much more comprehensive of his strengths and weaknesses, accepts his limits, and is able to see a light at the end of the tunnel, even in the most frustrating moments. All of the above has led him to have better control and feel better about life, and he has become more emotionally stable than he was.

There are many reflexology maps available on the Internet. After we came back from China, I did massage for both my husband and my son based on one of the maps, and it not only help their breathing but improved my son's gastrointestinal problem immensely.

The ancestor who discovered the connection between our feet and our body parts is a genius. It is so much easier to deal with our small feet than our whole body, and the excruciating pain every day for about twenty minutes is nothing compared to the long lasting suffering of chronic diseases.

You may wonder why I have such faith in reflexology. It goes back to my experience of witnessing one case in Brother Mountain's clinic that convinced me of the connection between our feet and body parts. One patient who had surgery to remove a brain tumor had taken a four-hour train ride to come for his treatment. The first time when I saw him, his big toe, which relates to the brain on the map, had reflected a round-shaped bruise with a very deep color after his surgery. It had become unnoticeable after almost three months of intensive treatment. His brain function had also improved immensely, and he was no longer nauseous, had headaches, or experienced confusion. He went back to his work before we left Taiwan.

Brother Mountain has also cured some patients who were abandoned by mainstream doctors, including a sufferer of an eye disease who was declared blind for life, a lady with a dysfunctional spine who was told she would be paralyzed for the rest of her life, and one patient with an extremely strange illness who all of a sudden woke up in the morning only able to walk backwards.

MIND

I believe no one would argue that the mind state of each individual not only affects his own life but also impacts his society immeasurably. Before my son was diagnosed, the neuro-typical expectation from others, along with the undetected war within his own body, had burdened him so much that he showed perceived "rebellious" behavior. He felt that the whole world was against him, even after the diagnosis had led to much more understanding and support from us. At that point, I realized that the only thing we could do was to help him change his own mind set, because it is impossible to change the mind set of others.

Changing his mind set was actually the focus during our yearlong trip. It is not easy at all with even a reasonable, rational child, not to mention one that has the unique mind of someone with Asperger's with resentfulness for the world and a lack of ability to express his feelings. If not for the guidance from my years spent learning about Buddhism from Master Chin Kung, the most respected Pure Land Buddhism teacher nowadays, I don't think I could have done this at all.

Of course, resistance from my son was expected, but the people we met in China shared more ancient values than the previous society he had been exposed to. This environment change constrained his defiant attitude and eventually he slowly accepted "sage teaching". The most progress he made was during the three months when we resided in a rental apartment in Hualien, which provided us a settled environment to watch Master Chin Kung's DVDs intensely.

The main idea of his teaching is *your thinking creates your world.* It explains the idea of "Cause and Effect", that *your thinking* is the cause that forms the effect-*your world.* It seems to be quite a simple concept, and you may interpret it and respond with "Well, good, if I think of becoming a millionaire, then I should be one then." Unfortunately, this does not seem to be true in reality, when some people work so hard and dream so big, yet never become millionaires.

It may bring a better picture to mind if we integrate this concept with the phrase "you are what you eat". For instance, the pear-shaped body is not caused by eating a lot of pears; indeed, the pears may lead you to a fitter figure because of their healthy ingredients. Conversely, a great deal of hormone-polluted products, even though they are advertised as being able to offer a healthy or sexy image, may lead you to an opposite end. Therefore, to examine the "ingredients" of your thinking is the key to understanding the law of "Cause and Effect". Thinking about becoming a millionaire, if it is for a selfish reason, the cause is actually "greediness", which, according to Buddhism, will have a disastrous effect on your life, even if you earned the goal.

Greediness, anger or hatred, and ignorance are categorized as "three poisons" to us according to Buddha's teaching. They deteriorate our souls and tempt us to do things that benefit only ourselves; in the long term, that benefit will just turn into a disadvantage or misfortune.

In my son's case, the frustration, the anger, and the resentfulness had worsened his situation, yet he had denied them all because there was no *scientific evidence.* No matter how I tried to share what I had learned with him, he ridiculed my ideas. I do not think it would be possible to help him change his attitude without transferring him to a different environment.

Thanks to the great land and the people of China, my son witnessed different values and gradually saw the benefits of the profound culture and its sage teachings. Without the influence of environment, I would have been unable to help my son to the path toward purifying his mind through the DVDs of Master Chin Kung's teachings, who introduced the profound ideas of Buddhism in a deep yet clear method.

The lack of scientific evidence is the element that stops many people, including myself, from embracing Buddha's teaching. I regarded it as superstition until about seven years ago. Intolerant to my mother's miserable life who had lain in bed from a stroke for more than twenty years, I started to search for a way to help my mother after all the medical treatments had left her in worse condition. I turned to a mysterious power, a variety of religions beyond human capacity to understand, and found that Buddhism has solved all my doubt and satisfied all my curiosity, including offering very "scientific" theories to my questions.

For example, in the Diamond Sutra, they have mentioned five different eyes, the naked eyes, the heaven beings eyes, the dharma eyes, the wisdom eyes, and the

Buddha eyes. We, as human beings, have only naked eyes; therefore, what we can see is very limited in this complicated universe. Buddhas, however, regain their ability through purifying the mind to ultimate perfection, and can see the whole universe clearly through five different kind of eyes mentioned above, including the infinite past and future. If this sounds incomprehensible or ridiculous, think of the X-Ray or Sonogram or MRI, which allows objects that are invisible to the naked eye to be exposed crystal clearly for medical use. When I read one Sutra, which teaches about filial piety and instructs us that the favors our parents have done for us are so profound that they can never be repaid, it described every detail of fetus development. This was a shock to me, because the description matches the images of the best technological equipment nowadays. How in the world, three thousand years ago, would Sakyamuni Buddha have been able to give the exact description without any "scientific equipment"? Did his eyes have the same functions of a Sonogram? Our science has finally proved his teaching thousands of years after his presence!

When my sister told me about an incident that happened to her shortly after I started learning about Buddhism, I was completely convinced that Buddhism was not superstition, but was based on total scientific theories. My sister, one day, was getting ready to take her husband to the hospital for an X-Ray to make sure he had not fractured a bone after just falling from a chair. Her friend, who claimed to have "heavenly eyes", called at that very moment and told her that her husband was okay, the fall was caught by his mother who had been deceased for more than thirty years. My sister had goose bumps all over after hearing this. Coincidence? Not likely.

According to Buddhism, all sentient beings have the same self nature, which are no different from "Buddhas". We lost our self nature because of our poisons, greediness, anger, ignorance, pride, etc... The power and ability of self nature will be recovered once our mind is purified. The different degrees of purification lead to different levels of power. Buddhas have reached ultimate perfection and are able to see infinite past, future and the mult-universe; my sister's friend surpassed naked eyes to reach a heavenly power or ability, and he was able to see into different spaces and other realms.

Therefore, the concept of "letting go" in Buddhism is one of the most basic and important teachings in order to purify our mind. Let go of pride, attachment; let go of the "three poisons", and we may recover our self nature and regain our "power" gradually. This teaching completely conflicts with our education nowadays. We are taught to learn, to fight, and to earn, and there is never a moment when the wheel of competition stops, especially in this era of an information explosion. Our children have been pushed to exhaustion in this competitive world, and this almost leaves them no room for anything else. The same as our treatment for all diseases; scientists have been so busy inventing new "medicines" to intervene in our bodies and to conquer nature, regardless of the side effects, even going so far as to risk lives.

My friend strongly recommended to us to give my son drugs to help with his lack of attention. He was so proud that his son was a straight-A student with the control from the prescribed drug. Of course, my husband, my son, and I all objected to this option based on our past experiences, and after doing research, we suspected it might cause many side effects, and some deadly cases. We decided on a natural way to help my son recover his self nature. It will be a long lasting struggle, but we have faith through the learning of sage teaching. Besides, the instant effect that the human race pursues nowadays has led us all to a very dangerous fate, the environment has been destroyed and the earth has gotten sick. Some Scientists predict that the earth will be impossible to live on in less than fifty years. If we do not slow down and take a break from the competition, we are rushing ourselves toward destruction.

Dr. Masaru Emoto, a Japanese scientist, has spent decades experimenting with water, and showed that our mind can affect the crystallization of water. In his book, "Water Knows the Answers", Dr. Emoto described in detail the results of his experiments and theory. Using all sorts of different emotional words and different style of music to let water "see" and "listen", then froze the water rapidly to minus five degrees Celsius, and finally obtain crystal photos through a microscope camera, Dr. Masaru Emoto has obtained very interesting and consistent results. When hearing classical music or seeing appreciative words, the water crystallizations were neat, beautiful and gorgeous.

On the contrary, when the water was given heavy metal music or shown bad words, the crystallization manifested a distorted, chaotic mess. Clearly, through the decades of experiments Dr. Emoto has demonstrated how the power of the mind can change the molecular structure of water and lead to the different quality of it. These experiments have proven Buddha's teaching that animal, vegetable and mineral all have senses and are affected by their environment.

The crystallization of water not only has helped Dr. Masaru Emoto understand the mysteries of the universe, but also allowed him to reveal the answer to life. He pointed out, seventy percent of the human body contains water, its condition could be very different depending on the variety of messages it receives. Our own mind, where the messages come from, impacts our physical body most directly. Therefore, if you harbor good thoughts, all the crystals within our body will be beautiful and healthy. And the inner beauty of crystal water molecules, will shine through our body and present a bright, optimistic spirit and a healthy physical condition. Therefore, these happy, healthy minds will virtually affect the people and things in our world, even mountains, rivers and our planet. Buddha has taught us that natural disasters like earthquakes and floods, are caused by our impure wandering thoughts, and can also be prevented by loving and compassionate pure thought. If we accept this logic, the Buddhist teaching: "Our thinking creates our own world" will become easier to comprehend.

My son was paranoid and cynical before this one year trip. His physical and mental conditions and school performance were all deteriorating. Once he accepted the sage teachings, learned to let go of greed, anger, pride and doubt, learned humility, contentment, gratitude, plus by praying everyday in the morning, his physical and mental conditions have gradually recovered. This is because everyone's body is the closest material to self-mind, and is affected most directly. According to scientists, the good, loving and pure mind is much more powerful than an impure wandering mind; its "wave" (magnetic field) not only can improve individual physical conditions, but can heal our planet and Mother Nature as well. If one-third of the people in our world spends even just five or ten minutes each day to purify their mind, whether it is by praying, meditation, or even simply to talk to a tree, a flower or a bug, sending out love and compassion, these "pure, loving" minds will gradually soothe the wounds of Mother Nature, and prevent the destruction of the Earth. Facing the most serious threat of cataclysm of our planet in human history, isn't this worth to try regardless of whether we believe in it or not? With a little effort every day, we may save our planet, or at least change our own mental and physical health, why not try it?

CONCLUSION

I did not get the chance to read the book "*Healing Our Autistic Children*" until I came back from this trip. To my surprise, I found the concept of what I did to help my son exactly matches what the book describes. Dr. Buckley treated her patient in three aspects: detoxifying the body's system by using a gluten-free, casein-free (GFCF) diet, removing suspected harmful foods that are believed to cause chronic gut stress to many autistic children. Then she prescribed a variety of supplements to the children based on many lab test results to determine the level of nutrition that the body needed to improve their immune system. Finally, the hyperbaric chamber therapy allows more oxygen to dissolve into patients' blood.

Compared to Dr. Buckley's biochemical intervention, I simply used natural ways to detox and strengthen my son's physical system—consuming as much non-polluted food as possible and merely using non-additive natural foods as supplements, and finally the reflexology that reduced his nasal inflammation allowing him more oxygen. Just like the promise from Brother Mountain, my son's sinuses have recovered at least 70 percent without any side effects at all. Unfortunately, in the last chapter of *Healing Our Autistic Children*, Doctor Buckley mentions that her daughter developed a seizure at age ten, even though she increased her IQ by nearly fifty points. I wonder if it is possible that it was from the side effects of too many interventions to her body.

We human beings always think we are the smartest species on Earth, and we never stop dreaming of conquering nature. Ironically, the more we head in this direction, the more our earth, the only planet known to support life in our solar system, is in trouble. And sadly, the more we advance our medical industry, the more diseases appear and everyday more people are getting weaker and sicker. The newest statistics in 2011 show the population with Alzheimer's has increased dramatically in our society, which may have a great deal to do with what we eat nowadays, in my observation. Scientists are trying to figure out a way to prevent it, which usually means some new drugs will be added to our already overwhelmed system.

By practicing a simple life of complying with nature has enabled me to recover from a very bad allergy, including chronic hives, asthma, fatigue, and red, swollen, and infected eyes—that my doctor gathered his interns to study with a textbook in his hand. The secret is simply following the sage teaching of "letting go" instead of "adding in". Let go of the attachment and the pride, and let go of the three poisons: greed, anger, and ignorance. Even let go of your cravings for food, dependence on medicines, and you will experience unbelievable benefits. My memory of a visit to the doctor during childhood always came with some food restriction; letting go of something to allow your body to recover. Unfortunately, this kind of practice no longer exists and we tend to get a whole bunch of prescriptions to "add in" to our system instead.

After one year of eating mostly convenient processed food while we were away, my husband looked like he was carrying a basketball on his belly. I suggested that he have his dinner in the early evening or late afternoon, reduce his dinner by eating only soup or salad, and eat a bigger amount of good food for breakfast. In less than half a year, his cholesterol level has dropped, and his belly has shrunk significantly. He looks younger and healthier.

You may worry that nutrition levels become insufficient if we reduce our meals, but I can assure you that will not be a problem at all. According to Buddha's teaching, about 70 percent of our energy is wasted in wandering thoughts. If a person practices purifying the mind, he will need less and less food. This theory has been proven by many Buddhist practitioners who only consume clear liquids like water after noontime, and are still much more active and execute a larger workload than most people do. I personally also try to do the same; skipping dinners when possible has made my body feel less burdened and more awakened.

I hope I don't bore you, but if I do, my suggestion is to go directly to the source. After all, forty-nine years of Sakyamuni Buddha's teaching encompasses everything you can think of, from the origin of the universe to the millions of microorganisms in a cup of drinking water, from life and its environment in different realms to how to eat and dress in our daily lives and from ultimate science to ultimate philosophy.

You can find any answers you are looking for if you regard Buddhism as an education instead of religion, like the original Buddhism that our ultimate teacher,

Sakyamuni Buddha, had demonstrated. We call him the "original teacher," a teacher that taught us everything, straight down to the understanding of our lives and the relationships we have with other sentient beings and our environment, the multi-universe.

It is fascinating and joyful to be able to learn about our life and environment. One of Master Chin Kung's teachers, Dongmei Fang, the most respected and famous philosophy professor in Taiwan declared, "To learn Buddhism is the most joyful pleasure in life." Master Chin Kung said he was attracted by his words and plunged into the learning of Buddha's awakening teaching in his twenties. Now in his eighties, he has awakened millions of billions of sentient beings with his wisdom. I felt so lucky to be able to learn this profound teaching. It is like finding the secret code to the happiness of life. My son, through his somewhat forced learning, has experienced similar feelings as well.

Compared to the 1990s, the information and treatment for autism has improved immensely. There are much more options for all of the disorders that fall along the autism spectrum, including Asperger's and other learning disabilities. Through the journey of dealing with this modern illness, a diagnosis is most crucial and liberating. It offers you a light to see and understand where you are, and it leads you to recovery in the future. Otherwise, it will be like looking for a way out in a dark dungeon and bumping into numerous obstacles, leaving you with a life full of trauma. I hope my son's story can offer the general public some understanding, lead to a better tolerance for Asperger's sufferers, as well as increase awareness of a child's development. I hope my observations and experience in the search for both physical and mental recovery from Asperger's brings you a different perspective to life, help avoid a late diagnosis and the pain and suffering that my son and my family have gone through. Hopefully it may help you to readjust your steps or even the direction you are marching to.

—By Elaine Gallagher

www.ingramcontent.com/pod-product-compliance
Lightning Source LLC
Chambersburg PA
CBHW061347280526
45784CB00001B/164